Bessie
in Love and War

A hand-colored photograph of Bessie Pringle taken by George S. Cook of Charleston. This image was owned by Mary Chesnut. From the South Caroliniana Library, University of South Carolina, Columbia, S.C.

Bessie
IN LOVE AND WAR:

Selections from the Letters and Diaries
of Elizabeth Allston Pringle

EDITED BY
KAREN STOKES

Bessie in Love and War:
Selections from the Letters and Diaries of Elizabeth Allston Pringle

Copyright© 2025 by *Karen Stokes*

ALL RIGHTS RESERVED. No part of this publication may be reproduced, distributed, or transmitted in any form or by any means, including photocopying, recording, or other electronic or mechanical methods, or by any information storage and retrieval system without the prior written permission of the publisher, except in the case of very brief quotations embodied in critical reviews and certain other non-commercial uses permitted by copyright law.

Produced in the Republic of South Carolina by

SHOTWELL PUBLISHING LLC

Post Office Box 2592

Columbia, So. Carolina 29202

www.ShotwellPublishing.com

On the Cover: *A photograph of Elizabeth (Bessie) Waties Allston, circa 1860. Taken by the noted Charleston photographer George S. Cook.* From the collections of the S.C. Historical Society.

ISBN: 978-1-963506-36-5

FIRST EDITION

10 9 8 7 6 5 4 3 2 1

Contents

Introduction i

Chapter One:
1861 1

Chapter Two:
1862 39

Chapter Three:
1863 57

Chapter Four:
1864 77

Chapter Five:
1865 117

Chapter Six:
After the War 129

Chapter Seven:
Married Life 149

Chapter Eight:
Widowhood 165

Chapter Nine:
The Years Beyond 195

Bibliography 201

About the Editor 205

Introduction

THIS BOOK TRACES THE LIFE and spiritual history of Elizabeth Waties Allston Pringle, a woman raised in the high culture and wealth of antebellum South Carolina. It focuses on her experiences from 1861 to 1876—those years encompassing the War Between the States, her marriage, and her early widowhood. After the terrible conflict that wrecked and impoverished her world, she and her family struggled to survive, but in time, despite manifold troubles, she found great happiness in marrying the man she loved. His early and unexpected death a few years later, however, would test all her strength and faith. She took on the difficult responsibility of running two rice plantations on her own and would later become one of the most notable Southern authors of her time.

She is best known for her books *A Woman Rice Planter* and *Chronicles of Chicora Wood*. The first of these, published in 1913, was a reworked compilation of articles she had written for the *New York Sun* newspaper under the pseudonym Patience Pennington. *Chronicles of Chicora Wood*, published posthumously in 1922, was a memoir about her family, childhood, and her life during the war years of the 1860s and just afterward.

Dr. James E. Kibler, an author and literary historian, noted that Mrs. Pringle's story may have been part of the inspiration for Margaret Mitchell's famous heroine in *Gone with the Wind*, observing in his book *The Classical Origins of Southern Literature:*

Bessie in Love and War

With the strength and grit of a better Scarlett O'Hara, Mrs. Pringle superintended two large rice plantations until her death in 1921. She vowed not to lose her family land and move to the city, and she didn't. Margaret Mitchell knew her story from her papers deposited at the South Carolina Historical Society and from her two books...Her works reveal Mrs. Pringle to be a classically educated traditionalist living in an increasingly anti-traditional time. The focus of her life and work might best be described as faith and family, neither very popular today with those who shape public opinion.[1]

The two books she authored were autobiographical and made her story well-known, yet they left us with something of an unfinished tapestry, with some parts less detailed than others. Surviving in her family papers at the South Carolina Historical Society are letters she wrote during the war years of 1861 to 1865, diaries she kept during that time and for several years following, and a small collection of letters and diary entries written after her husband's death in 1876. These manuscripts, most of which have never been published, are the heart of this book. They illuminate aspects of her life which were not so richly explored in her published works and are supplemented by extracts from her books and unpublished family papers which serve to create a fuller narrative. Although nearly half of *Chronicles of Chicora Wood* is devoted to her experiences throughout the war and its aftermath, her letters of this period, as well as diary entries not included in her memoir, offer added details, and a more immediate record of her life during this traumatic period. Scholars have for the most part neglected to utilize them. This book also features never before published photographs of Bessie and her husband.

Elizabeth Waties Allston Pringle was born into a rice planting family of Georgetown District, South Carolina, in 1845. She was called Bessie and usually signed her letters to close friends and family this way. Her father, Robert F. W. Allston, owned a number

---

1 Kibler, *Classical Origins*, 228.

INTRODUCTION

of properties, among them a rice plantation on the Pee Dee River called Chicora Wood, a fine home in Charleston (now known as the Nathaniel Russell House), and a summer beach house on Pawley's Island. A highly regarded author of scientific treatises on rice culture, he also served as a state legislator, and as governor of South Carolina from 1856 to 1858. He was a deeply religious man, and politically, a strong adherent of Jeffersonian republicanism.[2] Bessie's mother, Adele Petigru Allston, was a great beauty of Huguenot and Scots-Irish descent, and a woman of remarkable ability and intelligence. Mrs. Allston's older brother, James Louis Petigru, a well-known Charleston lawyer and unionist, was highly respected and honored in South Carolina despite his unpopular stand against the secession of the state in 1860. Bessie revered her parents, and among other relatives, she honored her Uncle Petigru the most, along with a beloved cousin, James Johnston Pettigrew, a Confederate general who was mortally wounded at the Battle of Falling Waters (Maryland) in July 1863.

Bessie's eldest sibling was her brother Benjamin, a graduate of West Point who served throughout the war in various capacities. Next eldest was her sister Adele (often called Della or Dell), who married a Confederate officer in 1863. A younger brother, Charles, spent most of the war in boarding school, being too young to serve in the army until the last few months of the conflict. Another sister, Jane, often called Jinty, was five years younger than Bessie.

In a biographical sketch written by Margaretta Pringle Childs, a Charleston archivist and preservationist, she noted of Bessie's girlhood and education:

> At Chicora Wood, her family home on the Peedee, Elizabeth Allston absorbed the beauty of the woods and the rhythms of plantation life, listened to her mother's stories, watched her mother's busy life as dispenser of country hospitality and mistress of many

---

[2] Allston stated that he adopted this "political creed" in 1825 "from a conviction of its purity regarding the peculiar nature of our policy and the character of the elements of this great Republic." Easterby, *The South Carolina Rice Plantation*, 14.

slaves. At Pawley's Island she spent summer mornings reading and keeping a journal and afternoons on the wide beach learning to ride well. With her older sister, Adele, she had lessons from Mary Ayme, a graduate of Queen's College, London, a woman of independent mind and intellectual interests. At nine she was sent with Adele to an excellent Charleston boarding school kept by Madame Acelie Togno, whose mother Madame Guillon conducted a widely recognized girl's school in Philadelphia. Planters' daughters from other counties and states came to Madame Togno's where French and music were strictly taught and attendance at plays and concerts encouraged.[3]

Bessie wrote extensively about her childhood in *Chronicles of Chicora Wood*. In this engaging memoir, she recounted two incidents in her early years when she was punished by her father, one of which involved a temper tantrum. On both occasions, she afterwards felt grateful for the punishment, understanding that it helped her in her struggle against a "poor, intense, self-willed nature."[4] She described herself at the age of nine as "a tiny child, small and thin, with deep circles under my big eyes, with an unusually alert mind, but shy and morbid by nature; very nervous and easily thrown into violent paroxysms of weeping by reproof." At Madame Togno's school in Charleston, Bessie recorded that she "wilted under disapproval and rebuke," but "responded to praise by redoubled effort." As for her later physical appearance as a teenager, she pronounced herself ugly, but recently discovered photographs of her as a young woman do not bear out this verdict.

Although she had more than her share of enthusiasm and vitality, like many teenagers, she was also given to periods of

---

[3] Quotes from Childs' biographical sketch are taken from a manuscript in her family papers at the South Carolina Historical Society. A revised version of this draft was published in volume 3 of *Notable American Women, 1607-1950: A Biographical Dictionary*.

[4] In her fine introduction to the 1991 edition of *A Woman Rice Planter*, Dr. Anne M. Blythe wrote that Bessie "was born with a passionate nature that needed and responded to a firm and constant discipline which she received from both her mother and father." Pringle, *A Woman Rice Planter*, xiii.

Introduction

self-doubt and self-reproach. Throughout her youth, when she was communing only with herself in her diaries, she sometimes gave expression to such feelings, while lamenting her continuing battle against a willful, high-strung, self-centered nature. In a diary entry of July 1861, she wrote of herself, "I am very dull and when ill nature is added to dullness, there's no standing it." In May 1864, she longed for the strength and ability to "conquer me, to conquer that proud, rebellious, impetuous self that is always ready to oppose any and everyone." The following month, she wondered, "if I shall ever be of use in the world, or if I am always to be the same cipher, the same useless nonentity."

Her writings, especially her unpublished letters and diaries, touchingly reveal how a girl who often considered herself inept, ill-natured, and useless, matured into a much-loved woman of exceptional ability, talent, and wisdom. Literary historian Dr. Anne M. Blythe called Mrs. Pringle's written record "the chronicle of a woman changing, a woman developing strength, learning fortitude, and growing in courage."[5] More importantly, she also grew spiritually, and it was this spiritual strength and understanding that gave her courage and enabled her to persevere through many ordeals and sorrows. In her sunset years, looking back on her life's "stormy path," Bessie saw how God had used all these trials to mold her into a person of deep faith and usefulness—a process she considered the central struggle and goal of her life.

The story of her sufferings and struggles during and after the war resonated with many readers when her books were published in the early twentieth century, but Dr. Kibler has noted that it still has significance for readers of today. The lessons of her life, he wrote, "can give courage to any and all, irrespective of time and place...Her message was that despite adversity, one soldiers on."[6]

---

5   Blythe, *Yours from the Wilderness*, 4.
6   Kibler, *Classical Origins*, 237.

Editorial Note

Almost all of the letters and diaries in this book are found in two collections at the South Carolina Historical Society: the Allston Family Papers, and the Elizabeth W. Allston Pringle Family Papers. The former collection includes her and her family's wartime and postwar correspondence, and the latter, her diaries. The documents were transcribed as written except for minor changes in some abbreviations, for instance, spelling out abbreviated words in brackets to indicate the full word. Ellipses indicate omitted passages. Brackets usually indicate the best interpretation of uncertain words or omitted dates, and a few illegible words or phrases are indicated as such in brackets.

Chapter One:

1861

THE FATEFUL YEAR OF 1861 would see the beginning of the war in America. The state of South Carolina had reasserted its independence on December 20, 1860, and soon afterward, other Southern states did the same, joining together to form the Confederate States of America in February 1861.

Bessie's first three letters were written from Charleston in early 1861, during a crisis which had been precipitated by the occupation of Fort Sumter by U.S. troops under the command of Major Robert Anderson. In late December 1860, about a week after the state's secession, Anderson had, by night, stealthily abandoned his post at Fort Moultrie on Sullivan's Island near Charleston and secretly moved his garrison about a mile away to Fort Sumter in Charleston Harbor. The South Carolinians viewed this action as warlike. The Confederate leaders did not want war, and over a period of nearly four months, the governments of South Carolina and the Confederate States of America sent commissioners to Washington, D.C., to negotiate a peaceable transfer of Fort Sumter, but President Lincoln refused to see these delegates, and they were unsuccessful. When Lincoln ordered warships to Charleston Harbor in April 1861, Confederate President Jefferson Davis made the decision to reduce (that is, neutralize) Fort Sumter so that it would be unable to join forces with the enemy fleet against Charleston. A bombardment began on April 12, and Bessie's fourth letter, penned on April

13, 1861, records the surrender of Fort Sumter to the Confederate forces, two days after which President Abraham Lincoln issued a call for troops for suppression of what he termed an "insurrection." The two governments were now at war.

While all these events were taking place, Bessie was attending Madame Togno's boarding school for girls (remaining in Charleston for the summer vacation period).[7] In early January she wrote to her mother at Chicora Wood.

> Thursday night
> [January 1861]
>
> My dear Mamma,
>
> You will be very much surprised to hear from me so soon but the boat has not left yet because of the weather. It is very unfortunate. Poor Will has been on board since yesterday morning in all this rain and wind![8] I hope he will not have another attack. I have had a very quiet time since you left but there has been a good deal of excitement down at the forts. A vessel has been fired into and Anderson has threatened to return the fire if the vessel is injured.[9] Margaret sent your dress home yesterday with the bill which I paid and enclose to you the receipt for fear of losing it.[10] I hope [she] got the dress to carry to you. It looks very nicely. Mr. Lance was better last night but not out of

---

[7] The scholastic year for Madame Togno's School for Young Ladies consisted of two terms, October 1 to February 15, and February 16 to June 30. It was located on Meeting Street in a residence now known as the John Cordes Prioleau House.

[8] This is likely a family slave named William. In *Chronicles of Chicora Wood*, Bessie referred to him as "William Baron." After the war, he became a well-known cook and caterer in Charleston. During the entire war he was the military body servant of Bessie's brother Benjamin Allston.

[9] In early January, James Buchanan, the outgoing U.S. president, decided to send a civilian merchant ship to Charleston to reinforce Fort Sumter. The ship, *Star of the West,* had armed troops and munitions concealed below its deck. The South Carolinians knew of its secret intentions, and sent a warning shot across its bow first, but then fired on the ship until it reversed its course and sailed away.

[10] Margaret was the maid of Bessie's sister Adele.

danger.[11] That is the message Aunt Ann got when she sent to Mrs. Bacot's.[12] I went yesterday to try on my dress. It fits very nicely. This evening Aunt May and I have been looking all over town for a pretty net.[13] The prettiest and cheapest I could get was $2.25, and as I could not afford that I have given up the notion.

With love to all, yr aff. daughter Bessie

Bessie's next letter of 1861 was written to her brother Charles, who was a pupil at a boarding school in Abbeville District, South Carolina.

18th February 1861
Charleston, S.C.

My dear Charley,

I hope by this time you have arrived safely and are quite settle [sic] down to your lessons. We missed you very much after you left and were very glad to get your letter written from Abbeville.[14] I went to spend Saturday evening with Helen Alston and had a very pleasant evening. I see Algy's company parading about very often.[15] Some of the girls myself included are going to try and make a flag for them. I hope Mr. Porcher liked your flag. Do you hang it out every day? Where do you hang it, on a tree or the lightning rod, or have you got a pole put up for the purpose? When you write do tell me all about it.

---

11   Likely the Rev. Maurice Harvey Lance (1793-1870), formerly rector at St. George Winyah Parish Church in Georgetown, S.C.

12   Aunt Ann was Mary Ann LaBruce Petigru (1793-1869), the widow of Thomas Petigru.

13   Aunt May was Mary C. Petigru (1803-1872), an unmarried sister of Bessie's mother.

14   Charles was a pupil at the boarding school of Octavius T. Porcher, located in Willington, Abbeville District, S.C.

15   Algy was William Algernon Alston (1832-1866). His company was the Jasper Guards, "a company of boys, probably of school age, commanded by Master Algernon Alston." Seigler, *South Carolina's Military Organizations*, 4:271.

The last news here is that Major Anderson is quite sick and that Dr. Geddings went down to see him.[16] I am very sorry for the poor man if it is true, which I believe it is. The Washington Light Infantry were relieved today from Morris Island. The regular Army take their place down there. Cousin Johnston and Hal have both come up but none of the family have seen them as they have been feasting at the Military Hall ever since three o'clock when they came up.[17] Papa is going into the country tomorrow morning. I wish he would not go but we have heard that the small pox has made its appearance in Georgetown. It was said there had been three deaths from it but we don't know what to believe. Papa thinks he had better go up and see about having all the people vaccinated. He is coming down again very soon, perhaps on Monday.

All send love to you. I hope you have quite got over you homesickness. Give my love to [Jimeni]. I hope his throat is quite well and now Goodnight.

Your affectionate sister,
Bessie

[P.S.] <u>Write soon.</u> I hope you appreciate this patriotic paper. I think it is very pretty.[18]

[April 1861]

My dear Charley,

I am quite ashamed of not having answered your two letters before, but times passes so quickly here

---

16   Dr. Eli Geddings (1799-1878), a prominent physician of Charleston.

17   James Johnston Pettigrew (1828-1863), Bessie's cousin, was colonel of the 1st Regiment of Rifles of South Carolina at this time. Her cousin Henry Russell Lesesne (1842-1865), called Hal, was in the 1st Regiment, South Carolina Artillery Regulars. He was the son of Henry Deas Lesesne (1811-1886) and Harriette Petigru Lesesne (1813-1877).

18   This letter was written on stationery that featured a color image of the flag of South Carolina.

1861

I am always so busy. Brother has gone back into the country but I will try and get the songs you want and send them up to you as soon as possible. We are all very much surprised at your having thought that Dela was engaged. She is not engaged and will not be for some time to come I hope. Where could Aunt Jane have heard such a thing![19] Last Saturday we all went round the harbor. I went with Madame to Sullivan's Island to look at the fortification there but all the rest of the family went with Gen. Jamison and they went to Morris Island as well as Sullivan's Island.[20] We all had a delightful time. I think I enjoyed much more than those who went round the harbor, for we (that is Madame's party) spent all the day down at the Island from 8½ A.M. to 7 P.M. I was not at all tired when we came home. You ought to see them, Charley. The whole island is fortified and all sorts of batteries are being put up everywhere. The men all look so well and happy, it is really delightful.

They say that Major Anderson is going to evacuate on Tuesday but they have been saying so all along and he is not gone, however, his provisions have been stopped and if he does not surrender soon he will starve. He has not had anything from town in the way of food for a week. Don't you pity him?[21] Algie Alston's company gets on finely. Madame Togno has made them a beautiful flag. It is made of silk, the Confederate flag on one side and on the other the name of the company, "Jasper Guards" and their motto "We conquer or die!"

---

19   Bessie had two aunts named Jane, Jane Amelia Postell Petigru (1795-1868), and Jane Gibert Petigru North (1800-1863). She is probably referring to the latter.

20   David Flavel Jamison (1810-1864), a lawyer, planter, politician, and author, was at this time the South Carolina Secretary of War.

21   Major Robert Anderson's provisions were stopped on Sunday, April 7, so Bessie's letter was probably written about five days later, on Thursday, April 11, the day before the Confederates began the bombardment of Fort Sumter. Since the latter part of January 1861, the South Carolina governor had allowed Anderson and his garrison to receive food and other provisions from Charleston markets. General Beauregard, the Confederate commander, ordered this privilege to cease on April 7, when it was learned that warships were on their way to Charleston Harbor.

worked in red and gold on white silk. It is very pretty but I am afraid it will be too large for [Roby] to carry.

Last Tuesday we were all very much surprised on waking up in the morning to find the ground covered with snow. Nannie came very early saying "Miss Betsy two feet of snow on the ground."[22] I, quite delighted, thought I wouldn't go to school so I jumpt back to bed to sleep, but I was again waked up by Jane, telling me that Papa said we must go to school. I got up in great haste and went down and found that Nannie's two feet had not been an inch and that there was no excuse for staying at home. I got to school very late, almost frozen, and found nobody there.

I am afraid this is a very dull letter, my dear Charley, but there is no news at all. Everything is as quiet as possible. Every now and then we have a great scare at hearing a great many cannon fired and we all run up on top of the house to see what is the matter, for we can see all the harbor from there, but we are getting quite accustomed to that even.

We will all write as often as possible and as soon as I hear any news I will write it to you. Something must happen very soon, for Anderson and his men cannot live without anything to eat, so you may expect to hear from me soon. All send best love and a shower of kisses myself included.

Your aff sister Bessie
[P.S.] Jim Carson is much better.[23]

On the evening of April 13, 1861, writing to her mother (who was likely at Chicora Wood), Bessie joyfully reported that Major

---

22   Nannie was a family maid.

23   James Petigru Carson (1845-1923) was Bessie's cousin. He was the grandson of James Louis Petigru (1789-1863), her mother's brother.

1861

Anderson had surrendered Fort Sumter to the Confederate forces. Looking out over the harbor through a telescope, she had watched all the dramatic events of that day from the uppermost piazza of her uncle's house on the Battery. Her next letter, dated April 14, was addressed to her brother Charles, and in it she reported similar details, exulting and thanking God that that the bombardment of the fort had resulted in a "bloodless victory!"

13 April
Saturday evening

Good news! Fort Sumter has surrendered unconditionally!! Ought we not to be very thankful my dear Mamma and as yet I have not heard of any of our men being killed. I did hear there has been one killed at Morris Island. Poor Anderson, they say half his men have been killed but they have fought very bravely and deserve credit as soldiers.[24] All yesterday and all last night they were pounded into by our guns on both sides; he stopped firing last night at dark, as he had no oil or means of light to see how to fire, while we continued all night, but he recommenced as soon as it was light enough and I believe Anderson is alive. Early this morning some of the buildings inside caught fire and have been burning ever since about 1 o'clock. Today a shot from Fort Moultrie took down their flagstaff but they immediately put up the flag on something else. Some time afterwards they raised a white flag, but without lowering the US flag they continued to receive shots from all quarters until at length they took down the US altogether leaving only the white. Immediately the firing ceased from the islands. All the men at Sumter directly came out on the ramparts and out on the wharf. I suppose the poor creatures were almost suffocated with the balls and shells constantly

---

24 Bessie was only reporting rumors here. No combatants were killed during the bombardment of the fort.

falling into the fort and their firing and worst of all the fire within. It must have been awful. We were obliged to send a boat from town to them, they were too much exhausted to come. I have not heard all the particulars yet so that I will not finish until I hear more. But one thing which makes us all feel not quite safe yet is that there are three war steamers anchored just outside the bar, supposed to be the "Powhatan" the "Harriet Lane" and the "Pawnee."[25] The [latter] made its appearance not very long ago but the other two have been there ever since this morning that can be plainly seen with the naked eye from the battery. One is a very large steamer and the other two are smaller. I have been watching the proceedings all day through a spy glass from Uncle Phil's top piazza and saw the US flag taken down and the white flag put up.[26] I have not heard anything of our relatives on the Islands but I feel as tho' they were all safe.

Sunday morning. I saw brother last night. Dear Mamma he is quite well, not having suffered anything except hunger. He came up to bring some despatches to Gen. Beauregard. He came round here for about half an hour and <u>eat</u> [sic] all the time. He sends love to all, says he is quite well and would have written to you but had not time. He has not slept since he left you but does not look the worse for it. He asked me to write home for him and you may consider this part from him. I am also to write to Charley for him.

---

25 These were warships sent to Charleston by Lincoln.

26 Uncle Phil was Philip Johnstone Porcher (1806-1871), the husband of Louise Petigru Porcher (1808-1869), who was the sister of Bessie's mother Adele Petigru Allston. According to the 1860 Charleston directory, the Porchers resided at 28 South Bay Street (now 46 South Battery Street). The third floor piazza would have afforded a fine view out over Charleston Harbor with Fort Sumter in the distance.

1861

I asked him what title I should give him. He said "Asst Adjt General!" Fourth hand man of Gen. Simons.[27] A great deal of what I said yesterday evening was false. There are so many reports out it is quite certain that there has been no one killed on either side and none even wounded on our side. The ships are still outside. Last night Captain Harstene went on board the Pawnee to take a passage on it for Maj. Anderson but I heard just now that he had refused to go on the US ships and wished to sail in the Isabella.[28] At present the fort is surrounded by the greatest number of steamboats, rowing boats. Anderson has been allowed to salute his flag before leaving and then our flag was run up and saluted. They say the fort is very much injured. Several fire companies spent last night down there working with their engines to put out the fire within but we will soon build it up again. I mean the fort.

Cousin Phil is quite well so [is] Hal.[29] It is the most wonderful thing no one being hurt. At Morris Island one man was struck in the back by a 32 pounder and was not hurt in the least. Another was knocked down without receiving the slightest injury! Marianna and Louise came down last night from the country.[30] M is suffering very much from sick headaches. I did wish so you were all here. It must have been terrible in your country, the suspense so great. Friday morning Aunt May and myself were up at 4¼ walking about the house in great distress at the continued fire. We went down to the battery a little after 5. From that time the guns went steadily all day. Aunt Ann did not stir until her

---

27   Bessie's brother, Benjamin Allston, was the Assistant Adjutant General to General James Simons (1813-1879), the commander of the forces on Morris Island at this time.

28   Henry Julius Hartstene (1812-1868) was an officer in the Confederate Navy.

29   Philip Johnstone Porcher, Jr. (1835-1864), was Bessie's first cousin serving as an officer in the Confederate Navy.

30   Cousins Mary Anna Porcher (1840-1875) and Louise (Louly) Porcher (1842-1861) were the sisters of Philip J. Porcher, Jr.

usual hour of rising. Aunt Ann and May [Clarissa] join me in love to all.

Your afft daughter Bessie

Sunday April 14 1861

Fort Sumter has surrendered unconditionally! my dear Charley after a fight of two days and a night. No one killed on either side! Is not this truly joyful and wonderful but as I suppose you have not heard an account I must begin at the beginning. First of all, Thursday evening about dark Andrew came round with a number of letters from home and saying Brother had arrived from the country.[31] You may imagine how surprised I was. I went immediately round to the house and saw brother who told me he had been ordered down by Gen. Beauregard to go directly to Morris Island. That night he left about nine o'clock. The next morning (Friday) we were awakened at 4 ¼ exactly by the most terrible firing of cannon! The attack on Fort Sumter had commenced! This tremendous fire from our batteries continued until 7 without response from Sumter, but it then commenced and fired shot for shot until dark that night when it stopped, not having any oil or means of light to see to fire. Our batteries continued to fire every twenty minutes during the night. All this time there had been three United States men of war anchored just outside the bar, the "Pawnee" the "Pochahontas" and the "Harriet Lane."

About 7 Friday morning Anderson recommenced his fire but not very strong. Soon afterwards the fort was discovered to be on fire by the dense black smoke bursting from every opening. This continued until about one o'clock (our batteries still pounding into S. all the time) when a shot from Fort Moultrie took down

---

31   Andrew was an Allston family house servant.

the flagstaff. The flag was immediately raised just so as to be seen above the walls. We still continued to fire, S. scarcely answering at all. At last they raised a white flag without lowering the United States' flag. Our fire redoubled and then they lowered the United States only leaving the white.

You cannot think the excitement it produced. I was watching all the proceedings from Uncle Phil's top piazza through a spy glass. I could see everything plainly. As soon as the United States flag was lowered the fire ceased from both islands and every man in Sumter was out on the walls in a minute. Poor creatures must have been nearly burnt to death. Just think from 4 ¼ Friday morning until about 2 on Thursday a constant fall of shells and balls into the fort and then the interior on fire![32] It must have been truly awful! Immediately little boats with white flags were seen plying about the harbor and the terms of surrender agreed upon. Anderson pronounced it unconditional and send [sic] up his sword and flag wrapt in a Palmetto flag to Gen. Beauregard acknowledging himself a prisoner of war! But Beauregard refused to consider him as such and gave him permission to leave when he chose and also to salute his flag; was not that magnanimous?

But could you believe that these ships were quietly looking on at all this. Anderson made a signal to them Friday and they might have come in that night but there they remained and saw there [sic] flag shot down and the fort surrendered without moving! Of course we thank them but we despise them for their cowardice.

And Charley does it not seem like a miracle, not a man even wounded! We ought really to be thankful to heaven for having delivered us from our enemies in

---

32   Bessie, who was sleepy while writing this letter, meant that the bombardment continued into Saturday, not Thursday.

such a miraculous way. Today Anderson saluted his flag before leaving and then ours was run up and he saluted it. He must be out at sea by this time. He was to sail in the Isabella for New York.

You have no idea what a military appearance the city has. The cadets are stationed on the Battery in camps and they have put up some mortars there for throwing shells besides the guns that were there before. Brother came up last night to bring some despatches. I saw him for a little while. He is quite well, not even scratched in the battle. He said I must write to you for him so you may consider this half and half.

I intended to write to you to tell you about the Cadet Ball which was very successful. I had a very pleasant time but so many exciting topics have arisen since then that I have no room for it. I wished so much you were here when all the firing was going on. It was so interesting to watch every gun and see from where it was fired. Mamma and all must have been so very anxious. They must have heard the guns and they could not suppose it to be what it really is, a bloodless victory! I have written as often as I could. I am afraid dear Charley that you will find this letter very tiresome. I daresay you heard it all already, but I thought perhaps you had not and a full account would be best. Goodnight my dear Charley. It is very late and I am very sleepy.

Your afft sister,
Bessie

The summer of 1861 would see the first land battles of the war, the most significant of which was the Battle of First Manassas in Virginia, fought on July 21. Numerous South Carolina soldiers participated in the battle, including Bessie's brother, Benjamin. It was a great victory for the Confederates, but South Carolinians mourned the loss of many native sons in this bloody engagement.

1861

Bessie remained in Charleston until sometime in August, when she traveled to her family's beach house on Pawley's Island.

Thursday evening
Meeting St.
[June 1861]

Many thanks my dear Papa for your kind letter and remembrance of my birthday, my sixteenth.[33] I will try and profit by your advice and the good examples you mention in Aunt Blyth and Cousin Lynch.[34]

Brother left us last night at eleven o'clock for Virginia. Mamma got a few lines from him this evening written from Florence to say that he had got that far safe on his journey. Cousin Phil left this morning for Savannah where he is to wait upon Commodore Tatnall.[35] Hal is over on Stono. He has got a commission in the State army much to Aunt Harriet and Uncle Henry's joy as he had quite decided to go on to Virginia as a private in the Washington Light Infantry, the company in which Henry Middleton has gone as a private and Cousin Johnstone expects to go in the same rank.[36]

Brother and I went last Friday evening to see the presentation of a flag to the Washington Light Infantry. Just before it left the flag was presented by Mr. T. Y. Simmons in the name of Mrs. Ancrum the daughter of Col. William Washington.[37] It is a beautiful flag but I

---

33   Bessie was born on May 29, 1845.

34   Elizabeth Frances Allston Blyth (1762-1840) was Bessie's great aunt. "Cousin Lynch" was possibly Elizabeth Allston Lynch (1728-1750), who was the wife of Thomas Lynch (1727-1776), a Georgetown District planter and an important figure in the Revolution.

35   Josiah Tattnall (1795-1871), of Georgia, an officer in the Confederate Navy.

36   Henry Augustus Middleton (1829-1861) was the son of Henry Augustus Middleton (1793-1887), a wealthy rice planter of Georgetown District, S.C. "Cousin Johnstone" was James Johnston Pettigrew, who, after serving as an officer in Charleston, enlisted in the Washington Light Infantry as a private. Originally a militia corps, this unit became Company A of Hampton Legion early in the war.

37   This was likely Thomas Young Simons (1828-1878).

should think was entirely unsuitable for active service as it would fatigue one man very much to carry it long. The scene was very impressive indeed. The company was drawn up in the centre of the Hall while the rest was crowded with spectators and friends. It was opened by a prayer from Mr. Porter then Mr. Simmons presented the flag and Capt. Conner made an excellent speech in return.[38] The men all seemed to feel the seriousness of the occasion. They marched from the Hall to the railroad and set out on their journey.

Mamma and Della have gone to a party at Mrs. Gen Brisbane's.[39] We went the other night to see Miss Ingraham and Mr. Whiting married.[40] They are going on soon to New York as he has a contract for building some railroad there and would lose everything if he did not go. There have been a great many weddings lately. Mr. Trapman and his bride have started for Europe, that is, they are on their way to Boston from where they are to sail, he going under the pretext of being Prussian Consul. But the most remarkable of the brides has been Mrs. Blake Heyward, who was married one Saturday night at 9 o'clock, went the same night to her own house, the following Friday gave a ball all on her own hook, for Mr. Heyward is a perfect nonentity. Miss Sally Huger is to be married next Wednesday to Mr. Calder. Dear Papa, I don't know if the weddings interest you much but there is nothing else to write about, everything is so dismal.

---

38 Mr. Porter was Dr. Anthony Toomer Porter (1828-1902), an Episcopal clergyman and a native of Georgetown District, S.C. James Conner (1829-1883), captain of the Washington Light Infantry, was later a brigadier general.

39 Abbott Hall Brisbane (1804-1861) was an engineer, author, and brigadier general in the South Carolina militia. He died in Summerville in September 1861. His wife was Adeline E. White Brisbane (1807-1872).

40 Jasper Strong Whiting, 1827-1862, an engineer and Confederate officer. He married Louisa ("Ella") Ingraham, 1834-1885.

1861

Madame is in great trouble as to where she will go this summer. She does not think at all of going North as she says she has cast her lot with the South. She cannot get a house in Summerville and has decided at last to stay here until Yellow fever comes. Della and I have been busy copying the music of Brother's song, have succeeded better than we expected. I hope you are coming down soon papa. We are all very anxious to get to the beach.

Good night dear Papa.
Your daughter, Bessie

The following month, Bessie's diary recorded the following entries:

Charleston, July 16th. I have just finished hearing Jane's French lesson as I have undertaken to teach her French this summer but unless we are both of us more patient I am afraid she will not learn much. I went today to tell Helen Alston goodbye.[41] She is going up to the Beach with Dr. Fishburn and John.[42] I do hope we will go soon but Papa left Friday to go to Richmond and he may stay some time and we will not go until he comes back and perhaps not then. We got two charming letters from Brother today he is in Winchester, Major of the 19th Mississippi Regiment and under command of Gen. Johnson.[43] He was expecting to march forward immediately.

Wednesday. Yesterday evening I wrote to Emma intending to ask Cousin Phil who is staying at the same

---

41   Helen Alston (1845-1918) was the daughter of John Ashe Alston (1817-1858), a rice planter. He had a son named John.

42   This was probably Dr. Benjamin Clay Fishburne (1835-1870).

43   Major Benjamin Allston (1833-1900), was temporarily assigned to duty with the 19th Mississippi Infantry Regiment, which at this time was in Virginia in the Army of the Shenandoah, under the command of General Joseph E. Johnston.

Hotel and who came to town yesterday to give it to her but he left very early this morning and I did not send it to him in time.⁴⁴ Capt. Lee came last night to tell us goodbye.⁴⁵ Della was taking tea with Anna Parker so that I had to entertain him. He has been very anxious to get away for a long time but could not be spared here. He was delighted at being relieved so that he can go to Virginia. He expects to go in Hampden's [sic] Legion. Cousin Johnston went to Virginia last week as a private but when he arrived there he was offered the command of a North Carolina regiment which he accepted and returned yesterday to make his arrangements and went off again today—he says brother's regiment is a very fine one. Mamma got a letter from Papa today. He did not say anything about coming back. This morning Aunt Louise and the girls paid us quite a pleasant visit.⁴⁶

I was late for prayers this morning. I really must get up in time tomorrow. I was very selfish too this morning in not going to Aunt Ann's as Mamma wanted me to and letting Della go instead. I am reading "Souvenirs of Madame Recamier" It is delightfully written. It gives very few of her letters but all the letters written to her by her friends male and female are given. I am now just in the midst of the Vicount de Chateaubriand's correspondence. She must have been the most charming, beautiful and best of women according to Madame Lenormant. Her powers of attraction and fascination were wonderful. Almost everyone who was brought in contact with her were charmed for life both men and women. Her devotion to Madame de Stael was remarkable in one so much sought after and flattered as she was—one would think that such a continued course of admiration, excitement,

---

44   Bessie's close friend Emma Cheves (1844-1910, who was later Mrs. Gilbert A. Wilkins.

45 Bessie inserted this note in her diary: "Gen Stephen D. Lee." This was Stephen Dill Lee (1833-1908), a native of Charleston who was later a Confederate lieutenant general.

46   This was Louise Petigru Porcher, whose daughters were Marion, Mary Anna, and Louise (Louly).

flattery and homage would have neutralized the better and hollier [sic] parts of her nature, but she seems to have remained through it all as pure and generous as ever. It really makes one despise Napoleon whom I have always admired to see his meanness and jealousy in exiling two such women as Madame de Stael and Madame Recamier from Paris. Madame Recamier during her banishment from P[aris] visited Italy, remained some time at Rome where she became very intimate with the two Canova, the painter and his brother the abbe. She afterwards went to Naples by invitation of the King and Queen M and Madame Murat and was treated with every mark of consideration and friendship by them. Madame Recamier was more intimate with Madame Murat (Caroline Bonaparte) than with any of the others tho' Lucien had been so very much in love with her long before as to write his letters from 'Romeo to Juliette.' The person whom I admire and love most in the book is Mathieu de Montmorenci. He is really charming. His letters are so pleasant and he is so good and true. He was devoted to Madame Recamier and was a true friend, encouraging her to the right and warning her of the wrong and dangerous. I have finished the first volume. I dislike Chateaubriand very much, that is I think him very selfish tho' I suppose that is to be expected in one so talented and distinguished. Still it strikes one disagreeably in his letters. In this they contrast very strikingly with those of Mathieu de Montmorency. It is delightful to know something of the private life of these persons named in history and who took so much part in the great events on which the fate of all Europe depended and those great generals Moreau, Bernadotte, Murat, etc., who aided in the elevation of Bonaparte and whom he in turn recompensed with thrones with the exception of Moreau, Bernadotte, King of Sweden and Murat King of Naples—all of whom were friends of Madame R[ecamier].

Thursday. This morning Madame sent Minna over with a message to tell me I must go there this evening. She is going to have the girls to meet to speak French. I daresay it will be very pleasant but it is raining hard now so that I am afraid that very few of the girls will be there. I was late for prayers again this morning and Acelie read me good many pieces of poetry that she has that are very amusing.[47] One from Cousin Caroline written accompanying a receipt for shrimp pie to Mr. Joe Dukes and his reply in which he thanks her for the receipt but adds that he cannot possibly read it. She had one little quotation from Sidney Smith that I wish to copy very much. She also read me two pieces by W. H. Hurlburt which were very pretty, one was really beautiful. I have not read any of Philip the Second for a long time. It is very interesting and I must not give it up but I was very anxious to finish Madame Recamier as Della borrowed it from Sabina Lowndes and I wanted to finish it before we went into the country which we intended to do tomorrow before Papa went. Della, Sabina, Rebecca Pringle and the two Middletons have made an arrangement to meet once a week at each house in turn to talk and read and be sociable.[48] They met today at the Middletons, and are to meet next Thursday at Rebecca's. It must be very nice. I should like to have something of the kind among the girls of my own age but it is so hard to start anything of the kind.

Isaac Hayne was here last night.[49] He was uncommonly dull and red. Della is going to drive with him tomorrow evening. I daresay she will be upset. I like him. I think he is a very good young man and <u>extreme-</u>

---

47   Acelie was one of Madame Togno's daughters.

48   Rebecca Brewton Pringle (1839-1905) and Sabina Huger Lowndes (1840-1921), like the Middleton ladies, were members of prominent Charleston families.

49   Isaac Hayne (1839-1888) was the son of Isaac W. Hayne, the Attorney General of South Carolina.

ly proper but dull! Since Minnie's sailing party when I behaved so badly he has only walked with me once. I'm sure I don't wonder for I am very dull and when ill nature is added to dullness, there's no standing it. I only wonder that he ever did speak to me for I never saw a person so utterly devoid of conversational powers as I am. It has cleared up and I must dress to go [sic] Madame's.

Saturday 20 July 1861

My dear Charley,

It is a long time since have written to you but I will try and write oftener in future. I have been very busy lately learning how to swim and I know how at last. Louise Porcher and myself were to see which should swim first so we went every day for a week down to the Bathing house on the Battery.[50] Louly learnt first but I can swim much farther than she can now. We got the gentlemen's bath twice. It is 60 feet long someone told me, and I swam it twice without stopping to rest or touching, which I am extremely proud of. The tide does not suit this week but we are going again next week.

The war news yesterday was delightful of the victory at Manassas but we are very anxious to hear something from Winchester where brother is stationed.[51] We have heard from him twice since he arrived there. He is under the command of Gen. Johnston. They are opposed by Gen. Patterson with a force double their own. There must be a battle there soon for they are

---

50 This was a saltwater bathing house that jutted into the Ashley River off White Point Garden. It was later used as the headquarters for the Confederate Signal Corps in Charleston.

51 There were skirmishes in the Manassas area in the days leading up to the major battle on the 21st, as well as an engagement in which the Federal troops were repulsed at Blackburn's Ford.

within eighteen miles of the enemy. We can only hope for the best. When he last wrote they were expecting an attack daily.

I suppose you have heard that Papa has gone on to Richmond. I suppose he will be back in a few days and then we will go to the beach. You know Cousin Johnston went on to Virginia as a private in the Washington Light Infantry but no sooner had they arrived in Richmond than he was elected Colonel of a North Carolina Regiment which he accepted immediately. He came back three days ago to make some arrangements, and to get his horse which he had left here. He is quite delighted with his regiment and says they are very fine men all of them. He also says that brother's regiment is composed of very fine men.

Mamma sent on William to brother just before he left Richmond. Papa was in Montgomery at the time and as soon as he returned he sent on Frank with Fitzgerald. The last we heard they had reached Richmond in safety. Annie Weston gave a party last night of which the only pleasure was the <u>Supper</u> which was very nice, and which you may be sure I enjoyed, but the rest of the evening was very dull.

This letter is very badly written dear Charley and I am afraid you will scarcely be able to read it but it is so hot and the mosquitoes are so bad that it is almost impossible to do anything. I suppose you have plenty of watermelons. Here there are a great many but they are so high priced that we in these hard times can't afford them so that we have not had one as yet. There are two in the garden that I hope will soon be ripe. There are no peaches at all nor figs.

Goodbye my dear Charlie. Try to study and be cheerful and happy. We think of you very often. All

1861

send much love. I will write soon again. I remain my dear little brother

Your afft sister Bessie

In July, Bessie's father, Robert F. W. Allston, traveled to Virginia, arriving just after the first great battle at Manassas, and afterwards he went to the battlefield, where he sought to locate fellow South Carolinians General Barnard Elliott Bee and Henry Middleton, both of whom had been wounded. In a diary he kept, Allston wrote that he found Bee dying, and that he was with him when he "breathed his last breath." Allston then went to find the whereabouts of Henry Middleton, who had been shot through the left lung, but learned that he had been sent off the field of battle to a location five miles away. "So I took shelter in Capt. Vanderhorst's tent," he recorded, referring to Arnoldus Vanderhorst, his future son-in-law. The next day (July 23) Allston continued his search for Henry Middleton, whom he found "late in the day, not dying, but dangerous. I followed Dr. Erskine of Ala[bama] to the battle-field where the dead and dying presented an awful ghastly sight, men and horses. The Mercury must contain a description as I met Mr. L.W.S. on the field taking notes." Private Henry A. Middleton died a few days after Allston saw him.[52]

In her own diary, Bessie wrote about the battle:

> Monday July 22nd. There is glorious and at the same time very painful news. Today, we have gained a great victory at Manassas, but at what a cost! Bee, Johnston (not the General) both killed and numbers of those we knew killed or wounded.[53] We have not heard from or of Brother. We know he was in the battle but I only trust he has not been hurt. I think if he had been it would have been mentioned in the paper. Theodore Barker

---

52 Mr. L.W.S. was Leonidas W. Spratt, a correspondent for the *Charleston Mercury* newspaper. Robert F. W. Allston's diary is found in the Allston Family Papers (SCHS 1164).
53 Lieutenant Colonel Benjamin Jenkins Johnson (1817-1861).

and James Conner have both been wounded, their poor families to find <u>such news</u> in reading the morning's paper.⁵⁴ It is too dreadful! The loss on our side is estimated at 200 killed, 300 wounded, and so many of them officers. Many such victories will destroy us, but let us look on the bright side. We took Sherman's celebrated battery, so distinguished in the Mexican War as Ringold's battery. This is a <u>great</u> triumph. It has been so much dreaded. It was taken by Virginians. We must no longer think of them slightingly as has been since the affair in which the galant [sic] Dreux fell.⁵⁵ They behaved nobly at Manassas and saved Hampden's [sic] Legion from entire destruction. I wonder how Mr. Vanderhorst is. Is he alive, wounded or dead. It is awful to think of so many whom we have known so well may be no longer!

Mamma has just sent on a letter and small parcel by the Rev. Toomer Porter to brother. He was going on as chaplain. I'm sure such men must be very much needed. Dr. Ogier is also going on as surgeon.⁵⁶ I am very glad of it. They have none there but very young and inexperienced men. Papa is somewhere there, where we don't know exactly, safe I hope. Mr. Brian has been very kind, bringing us all the news. He came very late last night to tell us what had come by telegraph of the battle.

Tuesday. Still no news of brother. Mamma is very anxious as are we all indeed. It is so strange Papa being there that he should not telegraph to us. I feel so weary all the time as tho' I had been working hard while I have been doing nothing at all. Last night we had a dreadful

---

54   Theodore Gaillard Barker (1832-1917) served in Hampton Legion.

55   Charles Didier Dreux (1832-1861) of Louisiana was killed at Young's Mill, Virginia, on July 5, 1861.

56   This may have been Dr. Thomas Louis Ogier (1810-1900). His son, Thomas L. Ogier, Jr. (1837-1863) was also a physician who served in the Confederate army.

1861

time. Nelson was quite drunk.[57] Uncle Henry came in about bell ring and stayed a little while and said that he would go to the Bulletine [sic] board and see if there was anything more. After he left Nelson came and locked the gate and door without heeding at all the ringing of the bell. When he came upstairs I noticed that his clothes were all muddy just as tho' he had fallen on his side into the street. Mamma told him not to put out the light in the entry for Uncle H. was coming back, but he put it out about 11 o'clock. Uncle H. came, rang at the bell but Mamma was obliged to go down and unlock the door and gate for him. He brought us the news that Jeff Davis had commanded our troops in person and Gen. Scott on the other side.[58] This of course makes it a much greater victory than we had supposed—Scott's first defeat! The first time he has headed a <u>flight</u>, not a retreat, a <u>flight</u>. When Uncle H. left we rang and rang but no one came. Mamma went and locked the gate and bolted the door and then went into the pantry to look for Nelson. She found him fast asleep in the back door. She tried to wake him up, called, and at last took a stick and pushed him but all in vain. Then as there was no one to be seen Mamma wanted to put out the lights herself and leave him there, but I am ashamed to say I was very much scared and so Della and I woke up Nannie and sent her to call Joe. She went, had to wake him up and told him to shut up and so we went to bed. It was dreadful. I felt so miserable.

This morning he did not seem yet to be quite sober. Mamma said she would send him to the workhouse but he begged her pardon and seemed sorry. I really hope

---

57 Nelson was described in *Chronicles of Chicora Wood* as a mulatto "butler and house-servant."

58 President Jefferson Davis was present at the battle, but Generals Joseph E. Johnston and P.G.T. Beauregard were the Confederate commanders at Manassas. General Winfield Scott (1786-1866) was the commander in chief of the U.S. Army, but General Irwin McDowell (1818-1885) was the field commander at Manassas.

he will not do so again. I got a very pleasant letter from Sophie today which I must answer very soon.[59] She [sic] been sick with neuralgia. She says she is working for the soldiers. I want very much to do something. I am doing nothing in the world. Last night I cut Col Dreux's last letter to his wife out of the paper to keep. It is really beautiful. I don't think it should have been published.

Wednesday morning. Elizabeth Grimball has just been here.[60] She had no news to tell but only came to see if we had any of brother which we have not. Gen. Bee's body is to be brought on today accompanied by a good many of his staff, among whom is Arnoldus Vanderhorst. I hope we shall see him for then we will hear direct from Brother. There is no mention of the 19th Mississippi regiment as having been engaged particularly so perhaps he was not in the fight at all. I should like him to have seen it if he was not at all hurt. Perhaps Papa may come today. We heard yesterday evening that poor Henry Middleton was <u>severely</u> wounded! It is very sad, he went forth in such spirits as a private. He tried very hard to get brother to go with him. I never saw him but that once when he dined here with brother but I liked him so <u>much</u>. His poor family! Mr. Pringle Smith and his father went on to him. His father had much better stayed at home. They do not agree at all. Young Ancrum has also been wounded but not severely.[61] His mother has gone on to him. His little sister "Mary Jane" is one of Jane's intimates and she went over to ask her mother to let her stay here during her absence but she had already left.

---

59 Sophie was probably Sophie Haskell (1845- 1922) from Abbeville, S.C., one of Bessie's fellow pupils at Madame Togno's school.

60 Elizabeth Berkley Grimball (1831-1914), who married William Munro in 1867.

61 James H. Ancrum, born 1843.

1861

Mr. and Mrs. Izard were here last night and paid quite a pleasant visit.[62] Yesterday it rained all day until the evening when it cleared up just in time for us to take a delightful walk on the battery. Louise has rheumatism in her legs. She went to bathe Monday and took cold. I am going to bathe tomorrow if it is warm enough, but yesterday and today everyone is obliged to wear winter clothes, very strange for the middle of July. Miss Grimball is going to give me some cuttings as I am trying to raise a small garden in my window but as yet have not succeeded very well. I have some morning glorys springing up very prettily. Jane brought the seeds from the Sweet Springs which makes them even more interesting than they otherwise would be. I have not been able to read at all or practise for some time. The excitement has been so great. I am going this evening to a meeting of the ladies for the purpose of working for the relief of the soldiers. I must really go and write to Sophy.

Thursday. We have heard nothing yet of either brother or Papa. I really feel distressed at it. Something must have happened. I am afraid, and Papa has not wished to let us all at home be too anxious, we could scarcely be more anxious than we are now. Last night we heard that Henry Middleton was dying, but this morning they say there is some hope. God grant that he may recover! His poor family, one brother is in the Asylum and the next, Frank, is very near it and this their only comfort and hope dying![63] But "hope on hope ever." Gen. Bee's body did not arrive yesterday but it is expected tomorrow.

---

62 This was likely Ralph Stead Izard, Jr. and his wife Esther Jane Read Izard, of Weymouth Plantation in Georgetown District.

63 Francis Kinloch Middleton (1835-1864) was mortally wounded at the Battle of Hawe's Shop in Virginia in May 1864. In the 1860s, his older brother, Cleland Kinloch Middleton (1824-1876), was hospitalized at the McLean Asylum in Massachusetts for "delusive fancies."

Friday evening. Oh! dear we have been to see the funeral procession of Genl. Bee and Col. Johnston. It was <u>very</u> <u>very</u> sad. The bodies were expected at 8 o'clock this morning but they did not arrive until 1 o'clock. We went to the Mill's House to see it pass on the way to the City Hall, which was all draped in mourning and where they were to remain until 4 o'clock when they would proceed up to St. Paul's church. Bee was to be carried to Pendleton and Bartow went on to Savannah and Johnston was to be buried at Magnolia.[64] All the Military in town was out, the hearses were not all handsome without plumes. The regulars came first after the band. They appeared really impressed and behaved with great decorum and solemnity. Next came the artillery and then the hearse containing Johnston. There were a good many officers on foot surrounding it, one of whom had his Scotch plaid wrapped around him. Then came two carriages and then another company who were followed by the hearse containing Genl. Bee surrounded by officers on foot and mounted, then followed by all the other volunteer companies with their arms reversed, the mayor and council and the Mounted Rifles leading their horses. There was very little solemnity in the behaviour of the volunteers at which I was very much surprised, for I certainly thought that gentlemen would know how to behave with due respect and deference while attending the funeral of their General, a man dying on the battlefield at the head of his men rallying them to a charge! Such a death is I suppose the one he would have preferred to all others, it [sic] certainly one covered with glory. South Carolina has suffered terribly in the loss of two such men, the country has suffered much! Oh how much is the death of such a general and his poor wife, what has she not lost, more than we can imagine.

---

64   Francis Stebbins Bartow of Georgia (1816-1861).

1861

Her case is particularly sad. She is from Main [*sic*] and has <u>two</u> <u>brothers</u> in the federal army.⁶⁵ What must her state of mind be and she is left desolate here. He was her only support. She is young and has two small children. It is dreadful to think of one in such a condition.

There is a report today that Henry Middleton is dead. Oh it is so awful to think of. Yesterday it was said there was some hope of his recovery. Can this terrible news be true? He was wounded in the neck. It would seem that such a wound would cause instant death. I can scarcely believe that it is so but none can tell what a day may bring forth. Nothing has been heard of brother or Papa. Yet I don't know what to think. It is very remarkable, not a word from or of Papa since the 15th and today is the 26th. Conjectures are vain. We must wait patiently and hopefully.

Arnoldus Vanderhorst has not come on. I am very sorry. I hoped so to have something direct and certain from Manassas to know if brother was there or not and what is the matter. But he has got another appointment and therefore remained. I should have thought better of him if he had come on. [Louis] was out in attendance this morning. Today has been a very sad day. Poor Mrs. Bee and Johnston, what a day for them. The minute bell has tolled all the time the procession was in march. It is still tolling. What a solemn awful sound it is. It strikes an awe to the heart when we think of all that now remains of those who not a week ago were in all health and strength. It reminds us of all those who suffer and die between its tolls; it reminds us how uncertain is <u>our</u> life and how liable to perish every instant and lastly how merciful is our Heavenly Father in having spared and blessed us with life and happiness until now.

---

65   Sophia Elizabeth Hill (1836-1920), a native of Maine, was General Bee's widow.

Hal came up today and says that Ripley thinks there will very soon be a descent on our coast.[66] This would be really terrific. Most of our men have gone to Virginia and many more are going to fill the gaps made by their last struggle and victory. We have had no list yet of the killed and wounded but so many who marched side by side with those who were out today have fallen it seems strange that they should not feel it more than they seem to.

I heard today that James Conner has been promoted to the place of Adjutant in Hampden's Legion and that James Lowndes has taken the captaincy of the WLI.[67] I am glad that J. Lowndes has shown himself a man. There was a good deal told about him before he went and I heard it would take a great deal of courage to silence it and show to the contrary. Henry Young is getting up a company of which he is to Captain and Henry Seabrook 1st Lieutenant to be called the "Dixie Guards." They wish to go to Virginia.

Madame had her French meeting last night. It was very pleasant. Lou Wilkinson played. She really plays beautifully. I went over to see the Grimballs this morning and paid quite a pleasant visit. I am going to walk with Louise on the battery so I must dress.

Monday July 29th. We have just come from the Bathing House where we have had a disgusting time. Louise and I went on Saturday and met Miss White who us [sic] that she and Miss Ingraham had been promised the boy's bath for today and asked us if we would not go which of course we did very willingly. We got there long before them.

---

66 General Roswell Sabine Ripley (1823-1887) was in charge of South Carolina coastal defenses.

67 James Lowndes (1835-1910), was the son of Edward Rutledge Lowndes and the great-grandson of Revolutionary patriot Rawlins Lowndes (1721-1800).

1861

Wednesday. Della and I have been to Henry Middleton's funeral. It took place at St. Phillip's [sic] Church at 4 o'clock this evening. It was very solemn. There was quite a large attendance. He died gloriously from the wound received in the defense of his country. Papa saw him the day after the battle. His wound was very severe. He had been shot through the lungs, but Papa said he was so patient and took it so quietly that he hoped the lung would heal. But God has seen fit to take him. His poor family, Alicia and Mrs. Hunter went on but I don't think they could have reached him before he died. I think it will be the death stroke to his poor mother, she up in Flat Rock with no one but Miss Harriet.[68] If it does not kill her I fear she will lose her reason which would be awful.

They sang the 33rd Psalm. It was very affecting to think of him as I last saw him in such spirits and health. But we must cease to think of the body now and only think of him as a spirit soaring on high and hovering watchfully over those friends left behind, think of him as "not dead but gone before." There was to be [any] funeral there at 4 ½, one of the Hamiltons, which I don't know. They did not bury Henry Middleton in the churchyard. I don't know where it is to be carried.

Friday evening. All day busy at Madame's fixing the house for the "fair" this evening from 6 to 10! What a time we shall have! Lou and I have the Raffles [List] to take care of, hers a doll and bed, mine a "Duchesse."[69] I was very sorry Madame gave me anything to carrie [sic] about as I <u>hate </u>to <u>beg</u>. Our utter destitution of money is really very painful. We really have <u>not a cent</u> that is we will only be able to pay our entrance that is

---

68 Henry Middleton's mother was Harriet Kinloch Middleton (1801-1878), who spent part of the war in Flat Rock, North Carolina, with her daughters Harriott and Alicia and other family members. Her daughter Mrs. Anne Middleton Hunter resided in New York.

69 A "duchesse" may have been a type of chair, or perhaps fabric or lace, or a runner.

10 cts. and none of us will be able to get a scrap to eat! It is so mortifying living in this large house, everyone thinking us rich. But let us hush complaining.

Yesterday Della's little sociable was to meet here. The Middletons did not come so that there were only Rebecca Pringle and Sabina Lowndes. They were very pleasant, Rebecca in particular. I like Sabina very much. I should so much like her for—ah, I must not be wishing nonsense, but she is so good natured and loveable. Her deafness is a great misfortune, but she bears it very patiently that it makes one like her all the more. Rebecca promised to send us a copy of a letter from Capt. Conner written the night after the battle of the 21st. She sent in [sic] the afternoon. It is a beautiful letter. I tried to copy it but it was too long. He speaks of Theodore Barker as having behaved "splendidly indeed." He says his conduct was too noble for praise; it was glorious!

Saturday. Papa arrived this morning. Della and I had not come down yet. He is looking very well tho' sunburnt, but says he does not feel well. He gives a very good account of Brother and says he is doing his duty like a man.

We had quite a pleasant evening at Madame's yesterday. There was a great crowd and we made $76 which is doing uncommonly well, I think. Aunt Lou and the girls were here today. They were very pleasant. I am quite distressed about Louise. I think she is not improving. She and Mr. Blake (Julius) go on too much together.[70] I wish very much that I could do her any good but I don't understand anything about good behaviour and never know what to say when she tells me her troubles. I feel for her very much. I understand exactly how she feels. I am afraid I would be just so if I had the temptations of

---

70 This was likely Julius A. Blake (1830-1903).

being pretty and admired. Last night she was constantly attended by L. Young and J. Blake and J.B. walked home with her.

I declare I love Mary Anna more and more every day. She is charming.

Friday. I don't know what I have been doing so that I can't take time to write but somehow time does slip away so we are going into the country Monday. I know we will not be ready when the day comes. Lou and I are going to walk this evening.

At the fair they collected the sum of $184 and since the Society has had an anonymous contribution of $10.

I have been particularly ill natured and out of temper for the last week. It is so horrid to be always answering disrespectfully and tauntingly which I do all the time and being so plain I think I might do something to make up for it. I try to be pleasant but I can't. Yesterday I dined at South Bay and Louly told my fortune by a book they have there. It was a dreddful [sic] fortune. Sure it was true in a good many things. One question, what sentiment do you inspire? My answer was "that of secret aversion. I was to marry for money a wicked man, be bankrupt and miserable, die at sea. No one regret at my death." It is very foolish to write all this, but I feel as tho' it was all true.

Beach. Monday August 26th 1861. I have been so lazy since we came up that I have not even thought of writing. Our journey up was very fatiguing but not as unpleasant as I expected. We stopped a night at Mr. Gaillard's in Plantersville.[71] They were very kind and hospitable and we had quite a pleasant time. We came

---

71   This was likely Sextus Tertius Gaillard (1803-1882). Plantersville was a settlement in Georgetown District which Bessie described in *Chronicles* as "a collection of houses built irregularly in the pineland, as summer homes for the rice-planters along the rivers." Their sojourn in Plantersville was usually from May to November.

over from there in a pouring rain. It was very cold for a few cold for a few days after we came up. Cousin Minnie is very sweet and little Jane is very winning but she has a tremendous temper and it should be controlled. Little Mary is the image of me! Poor child! My pen is so bad I must stop.

Monday, Sept. 9th, 1861. Della and I have just been to take lunch with Mrs. Weston. She is very pleasant, more cheerful than he was. Mr. W[eston] is better, she thinks, than he was.[72] We are going to dine with Cousin Min I must go.

Tuesday. Mamma and Papa have gone to Chicora today. Della has just got a nice long letter from brother. He is quite well and happy in his present post commanding the 8th Alabama reg[imen]t. It distinguished itself in the battle and having lost its colonel, applied for him to command during the absence of the other field officers.

Friday. Today Mrs. Ward was to have dined with us, but she has sent to say that [she] cannot come but will come and see us.[73] She has been quite sick with some kind of sore throat. Papa has had a sore throat for one or two days. Last night about 4 o'clock I was woke up by a whistle blown at intervals. I listened for about a half an hour and became frightened as it continued and at last I woke Della. Then I got up and went to the window to see if I could see anything, but I saw nothing. After a while I heard a groan from Papa's room below. I thought then it must be him wanting something. So we lit the candle and went downstairs. We found it was him and that he

---

72 This was likely Mrs. Elizabeth Blyth Weston (1815-1900), the wife of Dr. Francis Weston (1811-1890) of Hasty Point Plantation in Georgetown District.

73 This may have been Mrs. Joanna Douglas Hasell Ward (1805-1878), or the wife of one of her sons. She was the widow of Joshua John Ward (1800-1853), a Georgetown District planter.

1861

wished a poultice for his throat as he felt a sensation of suffocation. Dr. Hazel came early this morning.[74]

Since we have been up I have not read much. Mrs. Weston left me "Views A-foot" by Bayard Taylor. It is very interesting. It was written by him when a very young [brave] printer's apprentice and consists of his correspondence to different papers by which means he worked his way through Europe, all the expense of $500 gained on the way. He saw everything that was to be seen! Now it is such characters I like, and if I were a man, it seems to me "afoot" would be the way I should travel. Mrs. W. also lent Della "North and South," a novel it would seem very appropriate in name at least to the present state of mind, but it does not tell of our North and South but of that of England which I am surprised to find differs nearly as much as ours. For instructive reading I am trying the Rise of the Dutch Republic which is very interesting. I have not gone far but I do like William of Orange. So I have just read of his marriage to the princess Anna of Saxony. I ought to read it much faster but somehow I get on very slow.

Monday Sept. 16. Papa has been quite sick with sore throat. He is better this morning and has got up. Friday Mary Nesbit dined with us and in the afternoon we went to ride.[75] She rode Rabbit and I rode [Druse Allan] of which I am very proud. I like riding much better than I used to but I ride very badly. Saturday I go a delightful little letter from Aunt Ann. I wrote to her some time ago a short letter and her reply is so affectionate and nice. I have done my reading already this morning and am going to wash my gloves and mend my hoop.

---

74   Dr. Andrew Hasell (1803-1866) was a physician and a Georgetown District plantation owner.
75   This was likely Mary Nesbit (1844-1925), the daughter of Robert Nesbit (1799-1848), a Georgetown District planter who also had two sons, Robert and Ralph.

Bessie in Love and War

Bessie's last letter of 1861 was written from the Allston family summer house on Pawley's Island. From the beach, she could observe enemy warships patrolling the coastal waters. In one of her last diary entries for the year, she recorded hearing cannon fire which sounded like "distant thunder." This was the sound of a battle taking place over a hundred miles south down the South Carolina coast at Port Royal. A large fleet of United States ships arrived at Port Royal harbor in Beaufort District in early November and succeeded in capturing the town of Beaufort and neighboring areas.

This was to be the Allston family's last summer at Pawley's Island for a long time.

Beach 18 October 1861

My dear Charley,

We have just returned from the plantation where we have been spending the day. Papa left us on Monday for Columbia so that we are quite alone. We see the warships nearly every day. Today one was quite near in. Last night Mr. Weston (who is down at the camp near Georgetown) wrote up to tell Mrs. Weston that she must move over to the river immediately as he thought it was dangerous for her to stay on the beach, so that she is to move over early tomorrow. It is very early for her to move as it is not yet the 20th and that is the very earliest that it is healthy. I hope there will not be a warm spell or I am afraid she will suffer.

We do not think of moving over until the 1st November. By that time Papa will be back I hope. The plantation looked very pretty, indeed everything so green and bright. The vanilla grass is delightful. I will put some in here and you can put some in your desk and make it smell so sweet. I am sorry to tell you that one of your chickens had fits and died, but the rest are very well and flourishing. I assure you they are very

1861

bold indeed. You must know Jane has four cats all very nice and pretty. One of them is very large and fierce. When she feeds them you would think nothing could frighten them until one of your game chickens comes up and drives them every one away and then finishes the dinner himself. Is not that bold? He does it every day regularly and the cats after slight resistance go quietly away.

Dan your puppy is getting on very well but I must say Charley I think he <u>eats</u> entirely too much. He is a perfect object he is so stout, but he can fetch out of the water almost as well as Clara, so you see he is progressing in his education.

We haven't had many rice birds, that is not as many as usual, because Papa didn't want to waste powder to shoot them as it is very scarce. Harvest is over now.

We heard from brother not long ago. He is quite well and is still in command of the 4th Alabama Regiment. He says they a great many [sic] false alarms and are constantly on the go. He is encamped almost within sight of the Potomac not far from Manassas. He writes quite cheerfully but is in want of winter clothes, which Mama is getting to send to him by William when he goes back.

Della and I have been riding a good deal. The other morning I went on a fox hunt with Mary Nesbit and her brother. It was very pleasant. We went off early in the morning. We started four foxes and I enjoyed it very much.

Goodbye my dear Charley, your aff sister Bessie
[P.S.] Write soon.

Diary

Chicora Wood, November 4th 1861. We moved over from the beach last Friday in a pouring rain. Papa came over on Tuesday but we wished to stay as Mary Nesbit was staying with us and Mrs. Ward had invited us to spend Thursday with her. So he said he would go over Friday for us. Thursday was a beautiful day and we had a delightful day at Mrs. W[ard]'s tho' we did not get there until quite late. Alderly is a pretty place now and it will be beautiful when all their projected improvements are completed.[76] Coming over Friday we met two large flats containing the rifle cannon which Josh Ward ordered in Charleston and Huger Ward brought up to Kingstree. The two Magills and himself were poling away with the Negroes. Saturday there was considerable excitement on Waccamaw by the appearance of a steamer off the beach flying Spanish colors at half mast, within rifle shot of the shore. All the gentlemen assembled on the beach armed. The steamer sent a boat and three men ashore. As soon as they beached the boat they left it and made for the sand hills. Fortunately they were stopped before they reached them. They reported the steamer to be a coaster built in N.Y. for some firm in Cuba and said they wanted to see what sort of country it was. But the gentlemen would not allow them to go up the hills so they returned to the vessel which immediately steamed off. I think it quite evident that they were spies.

Thursday. All this morning we have heard steady cannonade as tho' from Charleston. It is a terrific sound. It is one continuous roll as if of very distant thunder. God grant we may defeat them. I suppose it must be that great fleet attacking Charleston or Port Royal. Brother's troop that was has been ordered out

---

76 Alderly was a Ward family plantation in Georgetown District.

this morning for active service so that we here on the river are almost alone.

Thursday Dec. 5. Papa has gone to Columbia again and we are here quite alone except for Charly whose school broke up some time before we expected. It is a great comfort to have him with us. I have had quite a bad cold. It is [over] now but I have a pain in my sides. I hope it will be quite well soon. I got a letter from Brother last night. I must answer it soon. I also owe one to Louise. [Marianna] and herself have gone with Aunt Ann to Badwell for safety.[77] We have not yet decided upon a retreat.

---

[77] Badwell was a Petigru family plantation in Abbeville District, S.C., and the residence of Bessie's widowed aunt, Jane Gibert North (1800-1863). In November 1861, Bessie's Aunt Ann (Mary Ann LaBruce Petigru) went to Badwell with other relations, including Mary Anna, Marion, and Louise (Louly) Porcher. Louly Porcher passed away from typhus at Badwell in December 1861.

The South Carolina Female Collegiate Institute at Barhamville as it appeared in 1860. Wikimedia Commons.

Chapter Two:

1862

BESSIE'S DIARY FOR 1862 opens with a lament for her young cousin Louise (Louly) Porcher, who had died of typhus about a week before Christmas 1861 at Badwell Plantation in Abbeville District. By early February, Bessie was writing from her home at Chicora Wood, and in March, she reported the surprising news that her sister Adele (Della) had become engaged to Arnoldus Vanderhorst.

Her letters begin in the spring of 1862, at which time she has resumed her schooling at Madame Togno's establishment, now in its new quarters at the South Carolina Female Collegiate Institute at Barhamville, located about two miles north of Columbia, South Carolina. Her sister Jane (Jinty) had now joined her as a student at Barhamville.

Increasingly alarmed at threats of enemy invasion, many of the planter families were leaving Georgetown District. Bessie's mother, and eldest sister Adele, took refuge at Croly Hill, a country house located near the village of Society Hill in Darlington District, South Carolina.

Diary

Jan. 10th, 1862. What a difference this short month since last I wrote has made in our family! Dear, dear Louise is gone, and so sudden and mysterious was her death. I do not, cannot realize it before we heard she was dead and had been laid in her resting place. So young and so very lovely and charming. Poor Marianna, Aunt Lou.

Feb. 9 (Chicora). I have allowed so long a time to elapse since writing here. I am so lazy.

Feb. 15. Helen is staying with me. Della and Papa have gone to Charleston and are coming back some time next week. Yesterday the papers brought very bad news. The Burnside fleet have taken Roanoke Island, shelled Elizabeth City, N.C., and are within a day's march of Weldon. Everything seems against us, but we must not give way to sadness. Of course we must suffer some reverses. Last night we took tea with the Westons. It was quite pleasant. We have not heard from brother since the 7th. He will be brought into active service by this attack on Weldon. Della got a charming letter from Marianna the other day. She feels truly that time alone can heal her broken spirit. How lone and dreadful she must feel. They expect to return to Charleston soon.

Monday Feb. 17th, Tuesday 18th. Sunday Mamma got a very pleasant letter from Della. They had arrived quite safe. They seem to be having a pleasant time. It has rained steadily for some time and is very cold. I have not finished the "Dutch Republic" yet but I will soon I hope.

March 10th Monday. Della is hearing [sic] Jane her lessons and I will try and write a little. Helen Alston has been staying with us for some time and I had no opportunity to write. I like her very much. Della came back from town with news which astounded us very much. She is engaged! To Arnoldus Vanderhorst![78] I am sure we might have suspected it for he has been devoted to her for a long while but somehow it took us very much by surprise. Mamma is very doleful about it; Della varies a great deal

---

78 Arnoldus Vanderhorst (1835-1881) was the son of Elias Vanderhorst (1791-1874), a wealthy South Carolina planter.

1862

and Papa and I are the only ones quite cheerful about it. I do not like him so much as some others, but if <u>she</u> does, I am bound not to influence her in the least so that I keep my opinion entirely to myself.

Brother is still in Norfolk and writes expecting an attack momentarily. We are all very anxious about him. He sent home Frank the other day. He only needs one servant and he keeps William. I want so to know what he thinks of the engagement.

I wrote to [M] yesterday hearing (through a letter from Cousin Phil to Della) that she was sick with a second attack of measles. I hope she will write soon.

I have finished reading the "Dutch Republic." It is very interesting. I wish had another as interesting to read. William of Orange is such a charming character, and Philip such a tyrant. The country struggles thro' so much and so gloriously it gives us encouragement to hope, but I am afraid our people are not so much in earnest as the Netherlanders were.

There have been a succession of reverses since Port Royal was taken: first the fall of Roanoke, Fort Henry, Fort Donelson, Nashville, Bowling Green and now Columbus. I fear Savannah will be next, tho' they say it will soon be impregnable. Fernandina too in Florida has been taken.

Cousin Johnston has been made a brigadier General much to our delight, for I don't think they can possibly advance him more than he deserves. We have been reading his book lately and is [sic] so charming.[79]

I have just read the Monastery and The Abbot and like them very much. It makes one love Mary Queen of

---

79 Bessie's cousin James Johnston Pettigrew was the author of *Notes on Spain and the Spaniards*, privately published in 1861.

Scots so much. She must have been so beautiful. I also read "Alone" which is an excellent book.

I was delighted the other morning to get a charming letter from Uncle. It was so kind of him to answer my note and made me feel very proud and happy.

March 27th Thursday. I have been lately very busy doing nothing! That easiest of all business. Mr. Vanderhorst has been paying us quite a visit. He arrived Saturday and left early yesterday morning. And Della is finally engaged. I hope it is all for the best, tho' I don't think it is. I don't think she cares enough for him. She certainly does not <u>love</u> him in the story-book sense of the word for of course that would be all nonsense, but I really don't think she likes him as she should. For my part if I had to choose for her it should be a very different sort of person. He is a <u>perfect gentleman</u> and nothing beyond; has no vices; is rather amiable, considerate, but not one spark of cleverness, no lofty aspirations, nothing grand in his nature, one who is entirely contented with the commonplace of life; no strong will, no determination. Della is as sweet and lovely as she can be, amiable, yielding, good and kind but lacks just what he does, will and resolution. It seems to me that in choosing that companion for life he who is to be a part of oneself, if one is not guided by love (which is seldom the case) one should choose a person having those qualities which we most lack. Therefore Della should marry someone with great energy, will, resolution, one who could sustain her, raise her gradually from that apathy and inertia into which she is too apt to fall, one to whom she could look up to mentally and depend upon for aid and support in the trials which everyone must expect. Arnoldus is, I think, her inferior in mental capacity. I think she would have been much happier with Pinckney Alston for tho' he was not so completely the <u>gentleman</u> he

1862

is more of a <u>man</u>.[80] But here I am writing about that which I have not right to interfere and I only hope I may have mistaken Arnoldus' character and that it is not so [yea nea] as it now appears.

April 17. Della and I went this morning to see Cousin Min.[81] It was a long, hot row but we have not seen her for a long time. We only staid to lunch and came back in time for dinner. Papa is expected this evening. I do hope he will come, he has been to Richmond. Brother was there at the same time on his way to join Gen. Kirby in East Tennessee. He will be now really in the midst of the struggle. God preserve him.

Cousin Johnstone [sic] has been made brigadier general. At first he refused the appointment, but this time he accepted. I am sure no office they could give him would be too high. I think he will prove one of the great men of this period. Our last victory at Shiloh was saddened very much by the death of Gen. Albert Sidney Johnston! He is a terrible loss, one which I fear can never be filled. He seemed to be so entirely a soldier and his wife and family in California, quite destitute. Many feel more confidence in Beauregard. I do not. I feel <u>confidence</u> in him, but not the enthusiasm, the love which I have felt for both the Johnstons. I hope he may realize all our hopes.

Fort Pulaski's being taken is very distressing. The idea of their surrendering without a man killed, and a garrison of five hundred. I really hope Emma has left Savannah for I think that must certainly fall.[82]

I have just finished three of Charles Kingsley's works. They are beautiful and noble. Amyas Leigh is

---

80 Thomas Pinckney Alston (1832-1864), the son of Thomas Pinckney Alston (1795-1861).
81 Cousin Min (or Minnie) was Mary Charlotte North Allston (1832-1906), whose husband, Joseph Blyth Allston (1833-1904) owned Waverly Plantation in Georgetown District.
82 Fort Pulaski near Savannah, Georgia, was captured in April 1862.

Bessie in Love and War

far the most interesting of those I have read.[83] It tells of the great men, soldiers and sailors of Queen Elizabeth's reign, Raleigh, Drake, Grenville and many others. And in Frank and Amyas Leigh are two pictures of men, lofty, noble, gentle, Christianlike men whose type is becoming alas more rare very day, I fear. But how can I judge? I know nothing of men anywhere but in this state and there may be many a shining light hidden for a time which will someday rejoice our hearts. Oh if the Almighty would make of ours a great and good nation! When we know that this is a new country brought into the world to take its place among the nations of the [hour], it behooves everyone to exert themselves to the utmost to make our men great and our women good. How every mother should keep in view that great and twofold end, her duty to God and her country. If everyone did their best, be it ever so little, everyone can do something, every soul must have some influence over another, if not another over their own, and in that is the first duty, and that no one can do without and every child of sin however weak can do something for the country in that. No government however great and wise can be sure of the blessing of God unless one and all, great and small, aid in the great work first by governing themselves and then all those whom God has placed under their influence. And oh may our Father in Heaven help me to do mine and that everyone could feel the importance of this, instead of blaming the powers that be for every misfortune that comes upon us.

The other two books "Yeast" and "Alton Locke" are very different from the first. They are written by an Englishman for the English and their object seems to be to bring before the rich and luxurious the true condition of the working classes and poor. They are powerful, and if [these] representations of misery and oppression

---

83 *Westward Ho!, or, The Voyages and Adventures of Sir Amyas Leigh.*

are true, then certainly slavery as it exists now is a thousand times preferable to the so called free labor of England. Kingsley is an Abolitionist but the reading of those two books has done more to strengthen my faith in slavery than anything else could have done. I have often thought it would be much better to abolish, not in the sense of the Yankees, who mean by that to kill the white man and make the Negro a murderer and thief, but that if there was any means by which they could get rid of them, form a colony of them or anything else, certainly we would be much happier. But after thinking of it and particularly after reading these books on the condition of the poor in England I have come to the conclusion that it is a divine institution. We know that there must be two distinct classes, the rich and the poor, in whatever form of government, and from all I read and know, the condition of the Negro slave is much better than that of the poor working man in England.[84]

Good Friday. We were startled by an invitation to tea last evening. Mrs. Starke Heriot gave quite a party.[85] It seems a bad evening to choose. But they say she forgot it was Passion Week. I did not think it quite right myself to go, but I am so weak I wanted to go. I found it very fatiguing. The truth is I am getting to lose my spirits which used to carry me through everything. I am apt to find things dull and add to the general dullness myself. We did not get home till nearly two! Today of course we went to church. The services are certainly very beautiful, but I find it daily more

---

84 On slavery, Bessie wrote in retrospect in her *Chronicles of Chicora Wood*: "When the Civil War came, the Southern planters were reduced from wealth to poverty by the seizure of their property which they had held under the then existing laws of the country. It is a long and tangled story—and I do not pretend to judge of its rights and wrongs. I have no doubt that the Great Father's time for allowing slavery was at an end. I myself am truly thankful that slavery is a thing of the past."

85 This was likely Martha Helen Ford Heriot (1837-1883), the wife of Robert Stark Heriot (1830-1875).

difficult to fix my attention on anything, particularly upon religious subjects. I do so long to be good, and it seems to become harder constantly. Truly the tongue is an unruly member. I did wish to be confirmed this Spring but I have not heard of the Bishop's coming and I fear so my inability to live up to what should be the standard. As long as we stay here it is much easier. But if we ever go to the city to live again and I should be surrounded by pleasure and excitement, I fear so I should give way. But I must strive to do my duty.

Sunday, April 27th. Mr. Hunter gave us his farewell sermon today.[86] It was very beautiful and touching. Everyone was much moved. I am distressed they are going. They leave Tuesday.

Tuesday, May 20th. I finished yesterday the only volume of Plutarch's lives which I can find. So that today instead of reading I intend to try and give an account of myself since I last wrote. Everything goes on as quietly as usual and the Yankees have not as yet given us any mark of favor. We will move to Plantersville next week I think.[87] Several persons move this week. The Middletons are at last to have the Tuckers' house. I am so glad of it. Yesterday evening Mrs. Charles Alston and Miss Sue called.[88] She looked very handsome. They are in great perplexity about a place for the summer

---

86 The Reverend Dr. Joseph Hunter (1809-1882), who had previously ministered in Brooklyn, New York, was the rector at Prince Frederick's Parish Church from 1848 to 1862. Bessie's mother wrote to Mrs. Hunter just after the war began in 1861 to express her dismay that Mr. and Mrs. Hunter's loyalties were with the North, not the South. Mrs. Allston wrote: "I cannot understand the madness which makes the North engage in a war upon us, whom they have professed to pity and deplore as the plague spot. Still less can I understand how you who have sojourned among us for 15 years nearly can join the [illegible] cry against us because we ask to part company in peace, and to enter into treaties for mutual understanding and good neighbourhood." Easterby, *The South Carolina Rice Plantation*, 176.

87 Bessie's father built a house at Plantersville in Georgetown District for a summer residence.

88 Likely Anna Washington Dunkin Alston (1829-1878), the wife of Charles Alston (1826-1869). They had a daughter named Susan Bethune Alston (1853-1936).

1862

and even applied for the Read's overseer's house at Plantersville which was refused them.

I have been reading a good deal lately. I have commenced reading "Alison's History of Europe" aloud to Mamma and like it very much. It is very long and the print very small. I hope we shall get through it. I was reading to myself the first volume of Plutarch which I found very interesting, but that is the only one here. It contains the lives of Theseus, Romulus, Lycurgus, Numa, Solon, Publicola, Themistocles, Camillus and Pericles, besides a life of himself. It is delightful to read of so many great and good men. I cannot decide which is my favorite. I am divided between Publicola and Themistocles.

June 1st. Mr. Shaw's near Kingstree.[89] Here we are run away from home by those horrid Yankees. Mamma and Papa are still at home and I wish we were there too. But we may never return there. It is awful to think of. Della has gone to church. I staid with Jane, who is, I am afraid, going to be sick. I do hope not. Yesterday Della got a delightful letter from Helen Middleton. She is a noble girl. I do love her. I got one from Em.[90] It was such a comfort. I am so afraid Em will forget me my letters are so dull. She has such a gay time, but she does not seem [to]. She is charming to me.

Mr. Shaw's, June 15th. It is Sunday again. They have all gone to church and I have time to write. Since I last wrote much has happened. A great battle has been fought and won but at what a loss! Numbers of our brave men have fallen, and there came a report that Cousin Johnston had been killed while leading a

---

89 This may have been one of the sons of Thomas Lynch Shaw (1795-1834), a prominent citizen of Georgetown. There was also a Henry David Shaw (1796-1866), who owned property in Williamsburg District, where the town of Kingstree was located.

90 Likely Emma Cheves.

charge and his body left on the field.[91] For three days the report was confirmed. I would not, could not believe it. Yet sometimes it came over me if it should be so, I should never see his noble face, never hear his voice and I could not think. It was so awful to lose in one year Louise who was as dear as a sister and then he whom I loved better than all my other cousins—but then the blessed news came that he was alive and out of danger and I felt how merciful our Heavenly Father is. Oh may I be thankful enough—in deed as well as word. Charley Porcher got through the battle unhurt. We heard of him through Mr. Vanderhorst and also one of his company was wounded and returned to his family in Kingstree and he told us of Charlie. He was well and in fine spirits. What a comfort it must be to Aunt Lou to hear from him such accounts.

Last night Della got a letter from Cousin Lou North that Cousin Min has another little girl born Thursday June 5th. The following Monday little Mary, who has been a great sufferer all her little life, was released from her pain and suffering to become a bright angel above. Poor Cousin Min, it must be a sorrow to her. I hope she will not feel it too much.[92]

Our Jane is quite well again. Adele and I find her very hard to manage. She is not a bad child but she certainly has been spoiled. Della has written to Madame to know if she can take us, Jane and myself, on credit or part of it in rice. I hope she will be able to do so for I am going back very fast and Jane needs a good school very much.

---

91 James Johnston Pettigrew was badly wounded at the Battle of Seven Pines in Virginia in June 1862. He did not die, but he was captured and made a prisoner of war.

92 Cousin Min, Mary Charlotte North Allston, gave birth to her daughter Louise Porcher Allston on June 5, 1862. Her daughter Mary Allen Allston, who was less than two years old, died a few days later on June 9.

1862

July 5th. Another great battle has taken place, more correctly a series of battles.[93] They commenced the attack on Thursday June 25, and when heard [sic] yesterday it still continued. McClellan's army was entirely defeated and in full retreat but not cut to pieces. Our loss is very great, tho' not so immense as theirs. There are many familiar names among the killed, both Grimkes and Robert Rhett, both so young, and Edward Cheves, only twenty one and an only son, and Major Augustus Smith, Sally Wardlaw's husband.[94] It is very sad. It is a terrible blow to her. She was entirely devoted to him.

We heard yesterday from brother. He has been ill for three weeks. He was moved from Taswell in the retreat in an ambulance.[95] He was fortunate enough to meet with a kind and hospitable family on the road who received him and have since treated with the most considerate kindness. It is a family related to the gallant Col. Ashby who fell in Va. The name of the gentleman is Cook, his wife was Miss Ashby and she has two sisters staying with her. I feel sincerely grateful to them and our Heavenly Father.

I have not written since before the fight on James Island.[96] Poor Henry King and John Edwards, they both fell covered with honor. John E's death was instantaneous, but Henry King lingered several hours.[97] Uncle writes that his death was that of a modest Christian

---

93   This was the Seven Days Campaign in Virginia.

94   Robert Barnwell Rhett (1838-1862) fell in the Seven Days Battles in the defense of Richmond, Virginia. Edward Richardson Cheves (1842-1862), the cousin of Bessie's good friend Emma Cheves, was killed at the Battle of Gaines' Mill in Virginia on June 27, 1862. Sarah (Sally) Wardlaw Smith (1839-1911) was the wife of Augustus Marshall Smith (1827-1862), who died on June 30, 1862, from wounds received at Gaines' Mill. Bessie may also have been referring to John Grimke Rhett (1838-1862), who also died at Gaines' Mill.

95   Tazewell, Tennessee.

96   This was the Battle of Secessionville on James Island near Charleston, fought on June 16, 1862.

97   Henry Campbell King (1819-1862) was the husband of Susan DuPont Petigru (1824-1875) and the father of Adele (Addy) Allston King (1844-1889).

and a gallant soldier and he died calling upon his wife and child. Poor Addy, she will feel it severely and so will Cousin Sue if she has any feeling left.

July 10th. I have just written to Em and hope she will answer it soon. Mamma got a letter from brother today. He is much better and by this time is with command [sic]. I am sure we feel very thankful to God for his mercy in granting his recovery.

August 23. The time approaches for us to leave for Madame's and I dread it more as it draws near. Our position there this year will be trying, I feel certain. Ellen Togno is married.[98] It does seem too ridiculous, but we have had no notice of it whatever and might never have known it had it not been announced in the papers. I heartily wish her joy, tho' I don't envy her.

Yesterday I got a delightful letter from Brother. He was at Tazwell and was in the fight there, acting on Gen. Stevenson's staff for the day.[99]

I have just read "Hertha" by Frederika Bremer. It is beautiful and very ennobling in its influence on the heart. Also "The Father and Daughter" which I read some time ago.[100] They present a great contrast in everything to D'Israeli's works which we have been reading, "Vivian Gray" and "The Young Duke," both of which are charming in their style but so much more artificial.

Soon after the above diary entry was written, Bessie and her sister Jinty traveled to Madame Togno's school at Barhamville together. It was at this time, as Bessie recorded in *Chronicles of Chicora Wood,* that she first took notice of John Julius Pringle,

---

98 Madame Togno's daughter Ellen (1843-1863) married Edward Wistar Macbeth (1841-1908).
99 General Carter L. Stevenson (1817-1888) of Virginia was in command of a division in Tennessee.
100 A novel by Ameila Opie.

1862

the man who would later become her husband. In *Chronicles*, Bessie wrote that this incident occurred in November 1862, but her diary indicates that she and Jane left home for Barhamville in late August 1862.[101] Bessie also stated that as soon as war was declared, Madame Togno moved her school out of Charleston, but in fact, she did not lease Barhamville until the spring of 1862.[102]

> As soon as war was declared Madame Togno moved her school from Charleston to Columbia, as every one knew it was only a question of time as to when the city would be shelled. She rented Barhamville, a well-known old school a few miles out of Columbia, and in November, 1862, my little sister and myself were sent there. The journey is specially impressed on me, for my elder sister had talked a great deal of Mary Pringle's delightful brother, Julius, who had left Heidelberg (where he had graduated and was then taking a law course) as soon as he heard of secession, and had run the blockade to join the Confederate army. She had been at home when he called and I had not, and she talked so much about him that I said, with my sharp tongue: "That seemed a strange way for a girl engaged to one man to talk of another, and wondered how her fiancé would like it if he could hear." She did not in the least mind this, but continued her praise, so that my opposition was roused; and, when, as we were taking the train, with packages and much impedimenta, our good Phibby[103] included, for she was to go with us, Della brought up the young man and introduced him to us, I said to her when he went to make some inquiry at the office for her: "So this is your paragon! You

---

101 An advertisement for Madame Togno's school at Barhamville that appeared in the *Charleston Courier* on August 17, 1863, stated that "School will be resumed on September 1st." The first 1862 term likely also began on this date.

102 News about her leasing of Barhamville appeared in the *Charleston Courier* on May 19, 1862.

103 Bessie wrote of Phibby in *Chronicles:* "The head nurse, old Maum Phibby (Phoebe), was a great personage."

certainly shouldn't choose for me!" However, he was a most attentive companion on the journey, and stood and talked to me all the way to Charleston, where we were to spend a few days before going on to Columbia. Jinty made me very miserable, because I was painfully dignified and speaking in the most correct and careful way, till I saw that while he stood and talked to me, she, on the opposite seat, was shooting peanuts skillfully into his coat-pockets. I could not speak to her and reprimand her, for she would have answered me back promptly, and I was terribly afraid he would turn and see what my little sister was doing. He did not, however, and must have been much amazed later to find his pockets full of peanuts.

13 September [1862]
Barhamville

Dear Mamma,

Tho' it is only a few days since you left, it seems like several weeks. Not that we are at all unhappy, but time passes very slowly. Madame is all kindness and has just been fixing our room as comfortably as possible. Jane and Minnie get on very well except that they get <u>ravenous</u> before dinner time. They seem very cheerful and happy. Jane finds the lessons quite hard but she will soon become accustomed to them. Nearly all the girls have come. There are now 37. They seem for the most part very nice girls. Kate Mortimer has come. It seems she left her Grandmother sick and tho' she has been here but two days I believe she is already quite disgusted. She cries a great deal, as indeed do all the new girls, so you may imagine that we are not yet <u>very gay</u>. Ellen Macbeth is staying in town with Mrs. Trenholm.[104] I thought I should miss her very much

1862

but Acelie is very kind. She asks me nearly every evening to go into Columbia with her and when it does not interfere with anything I have to do I always go. I hope you don't mind it, for she generally goes in the afternoon when we have finished our lessons and are walking in the enclosure.

I get on very well with my lessons and also with my music. Kate Withers who is in my class has arrived.[105] She is very nice looking, but I don't think I shall like her, however, I must not judge too quickly. Mr. Elliott to whom Madame wrote asking his services as chaplain has declined saying his health is too feeble, so that Madame is almost despairing. Poor Acelie suffers much from the exertion of her voice in teaching, and it is very much injured and Mr. Torriani says it will never be the same. Is it not dreadful? Of course she feels it very much. Madame hopes to engage a Virginia lady as English teacher. I hope she will succeed.

Yesterday evening I was very much delighted by the receipt of a paper directed to me in full. I suppose it must be good Mr. Bryan who was so kind as to send it. It is "The Southern Illustrated News" published every Saturday. I hope it will come again. It is so nice to have it to read today.

It contains a likeness of <u>Stonewall</u> Jackson, with an interesting sketch of his life. I do not think it is otherwise very ably constructed, but of course that is not much difference to us, as it is published in Richmond. Do if you know anything ask who sent it. Enlighten us on the subject if it is Mr. B (what made me think of him was I thought the direction was in his handwriting). I ought to write a little note of thanks.

---

[105] This may have been Katherine Boykin Withers, who died in 1865 at the age of eighteen.

Madame has put Phoebe to wash and Sara attends to our room. She is not half so nice a chambermaid as Phoebe, but she does very well [Jeemes] distinguishing himself in the brushing line. I take my first singing lesson today. I like Mr. Torriani very much as a teacher.[106] His little daughter has been very sick. I went in to see her and she looked and breathed so much like poor little Mary that it was really startling. She is better today and I hope will continue to improve.

A letter came from Mr. V. to Della and one today for you from Papa. I [hoped] to read the latter but Madame said I had better not so she forwarded it. Goodbye dear Mamma. Jane joins me in love to Papa, Della and yourself. I hope you have heard from brother. Do write soon and tell me all the news about yourselves and him, and believe me ever your affectionate daughter

Bessie

22 November [1862]
Barhamville

My Dear Della,

I think it quite shameful that you have not written to me this week. We got a letter from Mamma which was a great pleasure, and I almost think I shall have to say with Charley that Mamma is the most to be depended upon. Things have been going on as usual here. Min has been suffering very much from what we at first thought was neuralgia, but what Madame discovered to be a very bad tooth and made an appointment with her for the dentist today, so that the poor child has gone with her to Columbia. I am afraid she will have a dreadful time as she is in a very nervous state anyway having been suffering agony yesterday and

---

106 Born in Milan, Angelo Torriani (1829-1893) was a music teacher and opera conductor

1862

the day before, and her face is all swollen which will make it doubly painful.

This morning Mr. Macbeth arrived which is unusual as he generally does not come until Sunday morning, and soon after, I was startled by the intelligence that Mrs. Macbeth and Acelie were going on to Richmond with him on Monday. You may imagine it was a sudden determination but Edward is obliged to go on to Richmond on some business and he thought it would be a pleasant trip for Ellen so they are going to spend a few days and return. I have just been helping Ellen pack. She is delighted at the notion of going. Poor Acelie also very much pleased at the idea but she is just getting a stye which by Monday will be at its height and she does not fancy the idea of going in that disfigured condition, so that I don't know whether she will go or not. I hope her eye will be well by that time, so that she will be able to go with pleasure and comfort.

I have not been to Columbia for a long time. I don't therefore any news [sic] whatsoever except that Fannie Lamb has actually obtained a divorce from Mr. Lamb and married that man Geddys. Did you ever hear of anything so horrid! Ravenel Macbeth is also engaged to a Columbia girl Miss Pierson to whom he was introduced and became engaged the same night!![107] That may give you some idea of Columbia style!

I was very much distressed to hear of brother's being left in Kentucky. Then there is no hope of our seeing him this Christmas. I did so hope that he might come on and surprise you. It must have been a great shock to see William and the horses without him. Which horses are they. I thought Gerald was killed.

---

107   Agnes Wallace Pearson (1844-1911) married James Ravenel Macbeth (1839-1893) in December 1862.

Afternoon. At dinner Madame gave me your letter so that I take back all I said about you and writing. Thank Charley very much for his letter and tell him I will write as soon as I get a chance. I really feel for the Fords. It is very sad. I hope little Bet may recover.[108] Give my love <u>always</u> to <u>all</u> enquiring friends.

Min had the tooth drawn without the least fuss which is quite wonderful.[109] Dr. Reynolds said they had just gone in time for an abcess was forming which would have burst on the outside and disfigured her for life.[110] Is it not fortunate that she went today? She still is suffering with it very much as it is very much swollen.

It is delightful to hear such accounts from brother. I knew he would behave gallantly but it is so pleasant to know that his conduct is appreciated.

About what you say about it. My dearest I don't know what to say only do what you feel like. I sincerely hope A will not catch the fever. We have been having it very warm for the [sic] two weeks. Almost like spring weather, so hot and sultry. Give my love to Mamma and Papa and Charley and believe me your affectionate sister

Bessie

[P.S.] I find that the letter we wrote last Saturday has not gone yet and tho they contain nothing startling I will send them in this envelope.

---

108   Bessie is likely referring to the death of Stephen Charles Ford, who was born in 1853 and died in 1862. He was the son of James Rees Ford (1815-1889) and Martha E. Henning Ford (1819-1907) of Georgetown District. "Little Bet" was likely Stephen's sister Elizabeth (1859-1874).

109   This may have been Bessie's cousin Marion Porcher, who was sometimes referred to as "Little Min."

110   Likely Dr. William Reynolds (1807-1871), a Columbia dentist.

Chapter Three:

1863

AS THE YEAR 1863 BEGAN, Bessie wrote to her mother from Barhamville, anticipating the commencement of a new school term. In March, her family suffered a great loss in the death of her beloved uncle James Louis Petigru.

[January 1863]

My Dear Mamma,

Our holiday is nearly over and school commences on Monday for which I must say I am very sorry as we have had a much pleasanter Christmas than I thought possible under the circumstances; but Madame has been very kind and even Jane and Minnie have enjoyed it. But it is over now and we must return to lessons.

We have walked into Columbia several times for different things, and on Sundays and Christmas Ruth Nesbitt and I walked to church but Madame would not let the children go as it would make the walk too long to go in and return immediately. Acelie has been very kind. She is going to Charleston Monday to join Ellen Macbeth, who is having a very pleasant time there. Acelie is going under the care of Mrs. Devant (Mary Bostick) who is about my age and was with madame the last year I was with her. I hope she will have a pleasant time for she has been teaching so steadily that she needs some recreation.

I hope you received my last letter. Cousin Jane is in Columbia. She spent today with Madame. She is looking uncommonly well and [young]. She told me to tell you that she has had Uncle's letter and she thanked you very much for thinking of her. She leaves for Badwell Tuesday.

Goodbye dear Mamma. Give my love to all. Tell Della that I saw Olivia Middleton and she told me she was going to stay with Helen. When is Charley going back to school? I saw a most interesting account of the school in the Southern Episcopalian.

Believe me ever your aff daughter
Bessie

Barhamville
10 January 1863

My Dear Della,

Your charming letter has arrived and been fully appreciated. I assure you I should like above all things to have present [sic] at Beauty and the beast. I'm sure it must have been quite delightful. Plantersville must have become really quite spirited. Such gaiety is surprising. Every time I think of the beast and the proud sisters I cannot help laughing, It must have been funny. I am very glad you took the part as they all wished it. I'm sure you must have done well. Do if you have any more write me about it. It must be a relief to have papa at home again. Christmas must have been terrible without him. I hope the hands are all right now and that there will be no more trouble about them. I am sure it cannot be altogether their fault. They have behaved so quietly at home.

1863

I was really shocked to hear the account of Hetty Cary's being arrested.[111] It is truly diabolical. What will brother say I wonder. School has now been on a week, but all the girls have not yet returned. None of the Savannah girls have come yet. Acelie has not yet returned from Charleston. We expect her today. I hope she will come. The weather looks stormy. I miss her very much. She is so kind to me and I am so much with her. Jenny Bailey and I are going for her to town this evening.

Madame is very much occupied now as Miss Box found her health failed entirely and has been obliged to give up the idea of teaching and has left. Of course this gives Madame a great deal to do. Besides, one of the girls from Ga. is quite sick with rheumatism, Effie Stovall. She has a beautiful voice tho' she is only fifteen. It is very strong and as clear as a bell. You know that picture in "The Lays of a Lifetime"? She is very much like it with dark curls just like it. She is quite delicate but had been very well until she went home at Christmas and coming back she slept on the cars with the window open, a very cold night, and here she is in bed with rheumatism in both knees so that she cannot straighten them at all. She is an only child and a good deal spoilt so that it is a great trial to her to be here sick. Madame has written for her father. I hope he will be here soon. Madame lets me stay with her a good deal as she has no one among the girls friend enough to nurse her. Madame has moved her into Ellen Macbeth's room. Yesterday evening Madame sent me into town to meet Ella Wilkinson who was to come down in the Greenville train. I felt rather scared at going to the depot by myself,

---

111 Hetty Cary (1836-1892), who married General John Pegram in 1865, was a celebrated belle of Maryland. After the Federal occupation of Baltimore, she fled to Richmond, Virginia, where she spent the rest of the war. An arrest warrant was issued for her in Maryland because of her Confederate sympathies and covert activities, but she was never arrested until after the war.

but I was obliged to go as Madame could not and Ella did not know the carriage, but I got on swimmingly as the first thing I saw when the train arrived was Ella's face out of the window. I am so glad she has come. She is to be in Mad[ame's] dressing room, just next to us.

Madame just called me away to read me two delightful letters from Acelie. She is having a charming time. She is staying at the Mills House under Mrs. Beach's care. She has been visiting all the forts and altogether is as gay as possible there, a number of Frenchmen there besides the Gen. and staff. Gen. Beauregard and his aids give a great ball at the Hibernian Hall next Wednesday for which Acelie is going to remain until next Saturday. I am so glad she is having a pleasant time. I'm sure she deserves it. Madame is delighted at her having such a nice time and particularly at Gen. Beauregard's attentions to her. He wrote her a note requesting her to remain for the ball. She mentioned having been to see Mrs. Alston and says she seems heartbroken. Poor woman, I don't wonder. I was terribly shocked to hear Dan Petigru's death.[112] It must have been a dreadful shock to Uncle. It is the most terrible thing I ever heard of, such a sudden death!

I got a letter from Emma yesterday. She has been quite sick and I must write to her today. Give my aff[ectionate] love to all and believe me your devoted sister,

Bessie

Diary

Barhamville, March 8th 1863. It would seem as I took up this book only to record sorrow and bereavement in this family. So many deaths! But the sorrow which has now fallen upon us will be more widely extended than

---

112 Daniel Elliott Huger Petigru (1822-1863), Bessie's cousin, was the son of James Louis Petigru. He died on Jan. 5, 1863, from a sickness he contracted during his military service.

1863

any that has been yet felt. We heard yesterday that dear dear Uncle was too ill to survive the night.[113] He is at Judge King's.[114] Aunt Lou and Cousin Sue are with him and all his sisters had been telegraphed to. How I do hope Mamma may be with him at the last. It will be such a great comfort to her. When I think how kind and devoted he has always been to Mamma, taken [sic] the place of father and brother since sixteen. It will be a terrible loss to her, more terrible almost than I can realize for I have never felt the loss of a brother and papa who was so [sic] her real friends left and they are nearly all dead. I will have to mourn one of the noblest, truest, and best. But I know that both Papa and Mamma will be supported in this their sorrow by that peace that descends from above bringing the calming thought that all is for the best [for] his life has been a very long one and longer than the years has been its sorrow and its acts of kindness and love to all man, so that which is only a release for him leaves a sad blank in many hearts besides his relations.

14 March [1863]
Barhamville

My Dearest Mamma,

I scarcely think my writing to you at this time can be acceptable for in this calamity which has fallen upon the family you must be among the greatest sufferers, not but that all the sisters must suffer very greatly in the loss. Still it always seemed to me as if Dear Uncle was more <u>with</u> you and therefore <u>more to you</u> than to the others. It must have added much to your grief Dear

---

113 Bessie's uncle James Louis Petigru died on March 9, 1863.

114 Bessie is referring to the Charleston residence of Judge Mitchell King (1783-1862). His son Henry Campbell King lived here with his wife Susan Petigru King, the daughter of James Louis Petigru.

Mamma that you were not there at the last scene of his long and beautiful life.

I was much surprised and disappointed to see by the paper that St. Michael's had been chosen for his final resting place instead of Badwell as I had supposed. It must have been a great pleasure to see all the family tho' called together by such a sad occasion. How do they all look? I would think the one long year that has passed since you have all met must have wrought considerable change in some of them. Was Aunt May there also? Poor Aunt May, it will make a terrible difference for her, but alas it will make a great difference for all.

We were very much surprised by the arrival of Charley Porcher and his announcement that he would take Marion home with him to stay until the end of this month.[115] She was perfectly wild with joy. I am very glad she has gone just at present. She felt so anxious to be with her mother, so as to add her mite of consolation. Poor Aunt Louise. It must seem like the last drop in her cup of sorrow. It is fortunate for her that Charley got his furlough now. I was much disappointed to see him. He has certainly not grown, and as far as I could see not improved. I received the things to be dyed by [him] and Mrs. Macbeth takes them to town today to have [it] done. I have taken off the [border] to the shawl as Madame said it would be ruined by the dye.

Madame has been very kind to us. One day she allowed us to stay in our room entirely, and as it was cold gave us a fire. It was a great comfort to get Della's letter. Give my love to her. Goodbye Dear Mamma. Jane and I join in love to Papa and yourself.

Your devoted daughter
Bessie

---

115   Charles Porcher (1844-1913) and Marion Porcher (1848-1907), children of Bessie's uncle Philip Johnstone Porcher.

1863

25 April [1863]
Barhamville

My Dear Papa,

We were very much delighted to get your <u>two</u> pleasant letters, the last in answer to mine, for which I thank you very much, but you seem to think that I had not written before, when I had sent two letters before that one. Jane is quite distressed at hearing that Edith has left the house entirely and taken to the kitchen, however she hopes that her return home may have a good influence upon her. Chicora must be looking lovely now. I do long so to see it. This place looks much prettier now than I ever thought it could look. There are no flowers, but all the trees budding out make it look beautiful. I suppose there is nothing like a garden at Croley Hill.[116] Mamma must miss it very much. I am quite anxious to see Crowley Hill and Morden.[117] I know I shall like the latter very much. When I go home I want you to let me go with you on some of your expeditions up there.

This week has passed very slowly. The beginning of it Madame was very sick, ill, I think. She had a succession of the most terrible fainting fits caused by exhaustion and over exertion. For three days she was unable to lift her head from the pillow without fainting and losing her breath for some time entirely. Fortunately Mr. [Strock] was here and knew what to do for her. One night he thought her <u>very very</u> ill. Just as soon as she could sit up without fainting she got up and dressed and in spite of all remonstrances has been going on with school as tho' nothing was the matter, tho' I still

---

116   Bessie spelled the name of the farm as Croley or Crowley Hill, and in *Chronicles of Chicora Wood* described the dwelling there as "a quaint old-fashioned house set in a grove of oak-trees."

117   Bessie's father purchased a large planation at Morven, North Carolina, and moved many of his slaves there. It was located only about 25 miles from Croly Hill.

consider her quite ill. Acelie (who never showed to much advantage) nursed her faithfully while she was ill tho' herself suffering from her throat but as soon as Madame was up she was obliged to go to bed and is up today for the first time. I sometimes dread that this year will kill Madame as she says. The amount of trouble and worry that she undergoes is wonderful. Her English teacher and chaplain Mr. Johnson has behaved horribly, in such a manner as to forfeit all claim to the name of a gentleman, and it is only his holy office that protects him from open contempt. I am sorry to have to speak so of him but it is so.

Madame allowed Ruth Nesbitt and myself to take a walk outside of the enclosure last evening which we enjoyed extremely. Ruth is such a nice girl I know you will like her.[118] Do dear Papa when you lay in a supply of paper for yourself get some for me for I expect to have a good many correspondences this summer and I should like very much to have some nice writing materials. I should like the paper if you can get it about this size or a little larger without lines, both blue and white.

I got a nice letter from Charley two days ago. He seems to be improving very much. Certainly he writes very well. I was distressed to hear that Cousin Joe's eye was so seriously affected. I hope and trust he may not lose it. I hope they may not go to Plantersville while you are away. The time is rapidly approaching for us to leave school. Just think, Papa, I will leave school on my eighteenth birthday exactly. I am so glad for I wouldn't care to be at school after I was eighteen, tho' I must say I don't feel very well prepared to leave.

---

118 This may be Ruth Lowndes Nesbitt (1847-1884), who was later Mrs. Alfred Charles B. Holt. In *Chronicles of Chicora Wood,* Bessie called Ruth Nesbitt her "second great friend." She was from Georgia.

1863

Goodbye Dear Papa. Jane and Minnie join me in love. Jane does not write because, poor child, just at this time her Saturdays are spent principally at the dentist's.

Your affectionate daughter Elizabeth

Diary

Barhamville, May 2, 1863. We have just entered our last month at school for this year, mine forever. On the last day of school I will be eighteen. I really feel overpowered by my age and what should be my dignity. Friday night we had a May frolic which was a great success. Turner Macfarland was queen, Belle Smith crowner, Minnie sceptre bearer.[119]

[May 1863]
Sunday

Many thanks to you dear Della for having fulfilled your promise and written so soon. Min also got a letter from Annie the same day, so that our minds were quite relieved as to your safe arrival. I hope you have recovered from your fatigue by this time. After you left for a little while we felt quite doleful, but the pleasant remembrances of the visit soon got the better of all repinings and we have been quite joyful ever since.

Ellen Mordecai did not leave until Thursday, as it rained and was wretched weather.[120] She continued to treat me with greatest consideration and affection. She is quite anxious to buy those india rubber shoes brother brought as they are too small for me to wear

---

119 Ellen Turner MacFarland (1843-1930) was the daughter of William Hamilton MacFarland of Virginia. After the war she married John Wilcox Brown.

120 This was likely Ellen Mordecai (1837-1915), the daughter of Moses Cohen Mordecai (1824-1888), whose brother, Isaac D. Mordecai (1805-1864) was a Columbia merchant. Ellen Mordecai later married Jacob I. Cohen.

over my shoes. I want her to take them but can't bear the notion of being paid for them and besides have no idea of what is a suitable price. Just at this time I can't find one [foot] but I will look for it and send it to her. Yesterday afternoon I went to Columbia with Acelie and Ellen Macbeth. They were obliged to stop at the Mordecai's for something. Of course I did not get out (I never do when they go visiting) and I had sat there about half an hour quite contented when the door of the house opened and Ellen came running out saying in the most affectionate manner "Why Bessie my dear, you here. I had no notion of it until I asked A[celie] to stay to tea and she said one of the girls was waiting in the carriage and I was much surprised to find out it was you. Why didn't you come in?" I searched for an excuse and finally said that I was not dressed for visiting. She paid me quite a long visit in the carriage, kissing me on leaving. After Minnie came out with Acelie she also greeted me very cordially but to [clap] the climax [Pike] came out and with the greatest impressment shook hands and said "it was a very long time since he had had the pleasure of seeing me." When he has seen me oftener than I can count without taking the least notice of me. Rachel Lyons also came and spoke to me![121] Can you explain the reason for such a revolution my dear? For I am at a loss to imagine it. Acelie and Ellen are well. A[celie] sports her ring all the time and seems quite pleased with it.

You remember [Lida] Pickett (daughter).[122] She came to me the morning after you left with a sad face and said, "Oh Bessie! I should like so to know your sister. She is so strikingly like my Mother." Poor little thing.

---

121 Rachel Lyons (1838-1930) was the daughter of Jacob Cohen Lyons, a Columbia grocer. A celebrated Columbia beauty, she was the subject of Henry Timrod's poem "La Belle Juive." She later married James F. Heustis.

122 This may have been Lida Pickett (1847-1907), a native of Tennessee, who later married Theodore Clarke Caskin. She was the daughter of Joseph G. Pickett, a Confederate officer.

1863

I feel so sorry for her. Her little sisters in Nashville and her father ill in Richmond—is it not sad. Goodbye my dear. I am taking advantage of your last request to Madame and I don't want her to think that I presume on her kindness. Ruth has been sick since you left. Turner Macfarland is sick now, also Nell Villalonga.[123] Goodbye. Write soon.

Your afft sister
Bessie

[P.S.] How is your rheumatism and Mr. Vanderhorst. Do write and tell me. I succeeded in seeing Emma and thought her looking lovely.

After Bessie's studies at Barhamville ended in May 1863, she traveled to her family's home in Charleston to take part in her sister Adele's wedding as a bridesmaid. "The wedding was very beautiful," she recalled in her *Chronicles:*

> To begin with, Della was lovely beyond words, an ideal picture of a bride, and the groom, Arnoldus Vanderhorst, was a handsome and martial figure in his uniform, that of a major of the Confederate army. They were married by the assistant rector of St. Michael's Church, the Reverend Mr. Elliott, in our beautiful oval drawing-room or ballroom."[124]

Arnoldus Vanderhorst's "first groomsman" was his brother Lewis, a member of the Charleston Light Dragoons.[125]

---

123 This may have been Leonilla Dominga Villalonga (1837-1877), the daughter of John Ladislau Villalonga (1817-1880) of Savannah, Ga.

124 Bessie pasted this newspaper clipping in her diary on a page opposite her entry for June 27, 1863: "MARRIED. On the 24th ult., by the Rev. James B. Elliott, at the residence of the bride's father, Maj. ARNOLDUS VANDERHORST, P.A.C.S., to ADELE, eldest daughter of the Hon. R.F.W. ALLSTON."

125 Lewis Morris Vanderhorst (1830-1864) was killed in May 1864 at the Battle of Haw's Shop in Virginia. First organized in the 18th century, the Charleston Light Dragoons began as a volunteer South Carolina militia company, and served in the Confederate Army as an elite cavalry unit.

Bessie in Love and War

Diary

Charleston, June 27th. Della is married! It all seems like a dream. All the excitement is over and now for the first time I can think over it calmly. Wednesday at nine the wedding took place. It was a very beautiful ceremony. She was <u>perfectly</u> <u>lovely</u>. Her costume was a [dress] of plain dress [sic] of Brussels net (a beautiful material) over splendid white silk with a beautiful lace veil falling almost to the ground—a wreath of white hyacinths and bouquet de corsage of the same. Such was her costume but her appearance I cannot describe...

The following month, there was fierce fighting on Morris Island in Charleston Harbor, and the Allston ladies, seeking safety from a possible invasion, returned to Croly Hill in Darlington District. Mrs. Allston lived there for much of the war with her two youngest daughters and some servants while her husband stayed at Chicora Wood Plantation to keep it working. Della was also at Croly Hill for a short while until she left for Wilmington, North Carolina, accompanying her husband to his post there on the staff of General William H.C. Whiting. With the help of "the house servants" Mrs. Allston began to raise crops and plant a garden at Croly Hill. Bessie also kept busy, learning to weave and spin, and spending a great deal of time knitting.

Just before the Allstons left Charleston in July 1863, they received a visit from Poinsett Pringle, a handsome young man who left Bessie awestruck. Born in 1843, his full name was Joel Roberts Poinsett Pringle. Bessie described him in *Chronicles* as "the almost twin brother of my future husband," and wrote of their first and only meeting:

Before we left the city there comes to mind a very vivid picture of a visit paid by another member of the Charleston Light Dragoons, also a private. He was at home on a short furlough and called to pay his respects to my mother, and she sent for me to see him also. It

1863

was in the same beautiful oval drawing-room. Mamma was seated on the little sofa in front of one of the mirror windows, and when I entered the room, on a chair facing her and talking with great animation, sat Poinsett Pringle, whom I had never seen before, the almost twin brother of my future husband. Introductions were made, and I sat down and listened and looked, and looked and listened. Efforts were made both by himself and by mamma to draw me into the conversation, but in vain. When he had gone mamma said to me:

"Well, Bessie, if this is the way you are going to behave, you certainly will not be a success in society! You sat there with your mouth wide open, gazing at the young man! What was the matter?"

I said solemnly: "Mamma, he was so beautiful that I was paralyzed! I never saw any one so beautiful in my life."

And it was true. He was angelically beautiful; light-brown hair parted in the middle, with a curl in it, short as it was; wonderful blue eyes that looked like windows to a beautiful soul, fair, smooth skin, perfect teeth, and a dimple in his smooth chin—add to this very beautiful hands and the sweetest voice, and no one will wonder that my breath had been taken away by the sight of him. He was the darling and pride of his whole family. His mother had educated him for the diplomatic service. He was a most accomplished musician, playing beautifully on the piano, and had a charming voice. I never saw him again. All this charm and beauty of mind and body was snuffed out by a bullet the following May. I think it was the battle of Haws Shop in Virginia, which the Confederates lost, and had to give up the field. Poinsett was going out unhurt when he saw his friend Bee lying wounded. Poinsett picked him up and carried him some distance toward the rear, when a bullet struck, killing them both. If I could paint, how I would love to perpetuate that beautiful face and figure.[126]

There is an interesting passage in the diary of Judith B. McGuire of Virginia, whose brother, a physician, received a visit by a "young South Carolinian." The young soldier, named Pringle, had come to find the body of his brother who had fallen in a cavalry fight in May 1864. This soldier, who was almost certainly John Julius Pringle, had seen an account in a New York newspaper "given by a Yankee officer of several wounded Confederates." They had been captured, but died on the way to their destination, and had been buried on the roadside near the Pamunkey River. The doctor helped the soldier find the graves, one of which contained the body of his brother. They took up the body (wrapped in a blanket) and placed it in a coffin to be transported to a place called Summer Hill, where a funeral service was conducted by moonlight, reminiscent of "the burial of the lamented Captain Latane."[127]

Diary

July 11th 1863. Croley Hill. Yesterday morning about day-break a heavy firing upon the batteries on Morris Island commenced. As we were wakened by the sound the feeling was very awful.[128] Everyone rose immediately and I went down after a hasty toilette to find Mamma busy sending off some of the servants and their effects. We decided to leave at two o'clock. The preparations were very rapid and at twelve all was in complete readiness. Just before leaving I got a note

---

126 Joel Roberts Poinsett Pringle (born 1843) was severely wounded in a cavalry fight at Matadequin Creek in Virginia on May 30, 1864. He died in the hands of the enemy the next day, June 1. Bessie's niece, Susan Lowndes Allston, wrote that "his great beauty was even remarked upon by the enemy." Allston, "White House Plantation," *News and Courier*, Nov. 16, 1930. *The Burial of Latane* (1864), a famous painting by Virginian William D. Washington, depicted the graveside funeral of Confederate Captain William Latane.

127 McGuire, *Diary of a Southern Refugee*, 226-27. The diary entry is dated September 16, 1864. The body of Joel Roberts Poinsett Pringle was later reburied in Hollywood Cemetery at Richmond, Virginia.

128 Battery Wagner, Battery Gregg, and other Confederate fortifications on Morris Island in Charleston harbor came under heavy attack on July 10, 1863, and again the next day.

1863

from Hal entreating us to leave the city, saying things were by no means hopeless but the danger was imminent. I wrote to tell him that we were on the point of leaving. Poor fellow, he is at Cummins Point Battery. May God spare and protect him. James Carson came down from Summerville and volunteered in Capt Miles' Comp[any].

We arrived here Friday night at 12 o'clock. As we were not expected no carriage was at the Depot to meet us and we had the pleasant prospect of walking there until a messenger came in here to tell Daddy Aleck to get the carriage, but we saw a white [oval] in the darkness which proved to be John Williams who after having carried his sister home sent the buggy back for us.[129] Dr. Smith also sent his carriage for us so that we got home without much delay. People here are excessively kind, so kind, that it gives me a sense of obligation which I fear never to have a chance to get rid of. Everything that the nearest relatives and friends can do they do. Not only do they send things constantly but they come themselves to see us very often.

July 14, Tuesday. John and Connie were here last night and stayed until quarter of eleven.[130] We were sitting up for Arnoldus who was to come up in the Charleston train at eleven. He did not arrive until after twelve. Della and I dozed until he came. He will leave for Wilmington either today or tomorrow.

July 18th Sat. We received a letter from Della this morning from Wilmington. She writes very cheerfully, says their house is comfortable and seems altogether content. I am very glad to hear it. I had perhaps

---

[129] Croly Hill was the summer home of the Williams family. John Nicholas Williams (1797-1861) had also owned a plantation near Society Hill called The Factory. His wife was Sarah Cantey Witherspoon Williams (1810-1907), and they had a son named John Witherspoon Williams (1834-1914), as well as several daughters.

[130] Connie was probably Constance Williams (1841-1926), daughter of John Nicholas Williams.

foolishly feared otherwise. Everything goes on quietly enough here. Thursday I received three letters, one from Ruth, one from Marianna, and one from Hal. They were delightful. M's was very full of news from the city. It was very kind in her to write. I did not at all expect it. Cousin Phil is well but they can only communicate with him through the mail tho' his gunboat is in sight. They had not seen him at all since the attack commenced. Hal's letter was very gloomy. He thinks affairs <u>very nearly desperate</u>. His responsibility is very heavy as he commands "Battery Gregg" at Cummin's Point.[131] Poor fellow! May Heaven protect him in this time of peril. It was a kind affectionate letter, much more so than I deserve, so I answered it on the spot as he said it would be cheering to hear. Ruth's was like her own dear little self, full of affectionate faith and love. How unworthy I am of my friends Ruth and Emma. Emma is in great sorrow. Her father was killed at the first shell.[132] Poor child—she must suffer terribly. Her cousin Charles Haskell has also been killed.[133]

Yesterday morning [Causey] sent me a beautiful basket of flowers and a little apple geranium plant, which I like very much. I have just finished "Jane Eyre" and "Sylvan Holt's Daughter," both very interesting but entirely different in every way. I vastly prefer Jane Eyre.[134]

---

131   Bessie's cousin Henry (Hal) Russell Lesesne was promoted to the rank of captain in July 1863. The next month, he suffered slight wounds at Battery Gregg on Morris Island. He was killed at the Battle of Averasboro in North Carolina in March 1865.

132   Emma's father was Captain Langdon Cheves (1814 -1863), a Confederate engineer who helped designed Battery Wagner on Morris Island. He was killed on July 10, 1863, by a shell that exploded in the fort.

133   Captain Charles T. Haskell (1835-1863) was shot down on Morris Island in the same battle in which his uncle Langdon Cheves fell.

134   *Sylvan Holt's Daughter* (1858) was a novel by British author Harriet Parr (1828-1900), who wrote under the pen name Holme Lee.

1863

July 19th, Sunday. Just as we were leaving for church the paper came and therein was the dreadful intelligence that Cousin Johnston had died of his wounds.[135] It is too dreadful! If I could I would hope that this like the first may be a false report but something tells me it is true, and here I sit as quiet and composed as if nothing had happened. I wonder if I have lost all feeling, or what it is, I don't and can't realize it. Every feeling seems numb.

Next to Uncle he was the light of our family—so clever and learned, and so noble—and how I have almost adored him in his nobleness and wisdom. How I have sat and listened to Uncle and himself talking until I thought nothing could ever be as pleasant as that but now both have gone, and we shall never see their equals again. We hear he was wounded at Gettysburg but his name was not mentioned among the generals and never since, so we supposed it slight and now...

Just returned from church, had a beautiful service. Mr. Kidney is the rector here.[136] I like him very much, but today a Mr. Olmstedd preached.[137] He gave a beautiful sermon, not at all like a sermon. He seemed talking to us so earnestly that it is impossible not to feel. His text was "Be ye not troubled, ye believe in God, believe also in me." It is peculiarly appropriate to the present time when each and all have some reason for fear and anxiety. I must write to Della now.

After returning to Croly Hill, Bessie experienced a few more encounters with her future husband, the last of which was to be of

---

[135] General James Johnston Pettigrew died on July 17, 1863, from wounds received at the Battle of Falling Waters.
[136] John Steinfort Kedney (1819-1911) was an Episcopal minister and poet. He was rector at Trinity Church in Society Hill during the war.
[137] This was the Rev. Aaron F. Olmsted (1818-1895).

Bessie in Love and War

supreme significance in her life. In *Chronicles of Chicora Wood,* she gives no date for these incidents, but they likely took place in 1863.

> One day we had a visit from Julius Pringle, who was on furlough at the house of an uncle, who was refugeeing about four miles away. This was only the second time I saw him. Mamma and he did all the talking, while I sewed in silence. Mamma went out of the room to order some cake and wine, and he told me he didn't know the way to Crowley, and had come to a place where four roads crossed, and was puzzling how to decide which road to take "when I saw a track of a very tiny foot leading this way, and I followed that and I knew it would bring me to you." This made me very angry indeed, and I got red and lost the use of my quick tongue. When Mamma came back the talk flowed on as easily and pleasantly as possible. She told him what a fine crop of rye she had made in her calf pasture, and what difficulty she had to find a place to put it until she thought of the big piano box, which had helped very much, for it held so much. All this time I sewed in silence, with flaming face. At last he asked me to play. I declined fiercely, but mamma said: "My dear Bessie! Of course you will play for us"—she being quite shocked at my manner. I went to the piano and played as though I were fighting the Yankees. When I returned to my seat Mr. Pringle thanked me, and, turning to my mother, said: "Mrs. Allston, apparently the piano box is of more use than the piano!" And then they both laughed heartily.
>
> I could have killed him without hesitation. I saw him at church after that, only a moment. And then the day he was to leave to go back to Virginia, mamma wanted to ask him to take a letter, and we drove to the station. And when he shook hands with me and said good-by, the look in his eye was a revelation and

declaration of devotion that seemed to compass me and seal me as forever his, near or far, with my own will or without it. From that moment I knew that no other man could be anything to me. It was so strange that in absolute silence, with not a second's prolonging of the hand-pressure necessary to say a proper, conventional good-by, my whole life was altered; for up to that moment I had no idea that he was devoted to me.[138]

---

138   John Julius Pringle served in Company K, 4th South Carolina Cavalry Regiment (the Charleston Light Dragoons).

A twentieth century photograph of Croly Hill, built ca. 1820.
Courtesy South Carolina Department of Archives and History.

Chapter Four:

1864

IN EARLY 1864, Bessie spent a month or so in Wilmington with her sister Adele, and in March she returned to Croly Hill. Although she was happy her father came there that month for a "little longer visit than usual," she was unaware at the time that his health was in serious decline. He left for Chicora Wood on March 18, and about a week later, when Mrs. Allston received word that he was very ill, she and Bessie immediately left Croly Hill to be with him. When they arrived at Chicora Wood, they found Mr. Allston bedridden, suffering from congestive heart failure and pneumonia. He died on April 7, 1864. On April 11, Bessie wrote a poignant letter to her brother Benjamin, who was serving on the staff of General Kirby Smith in the Trans Mississippi Department, describing their father's last days and passing.

Diary

Wilmington, Feb. 26th 1864. I have been here a month staying with Della, and as far as her company goes, having a very pleasant time, but I don't suit company, particularly when composed of strangers. I realize it more every day. I used to think I would get over it, but instead it increases and I think I will soon be reduced to the society of none but my own immediate family. We have quite a number of pleasant acquaintances among the officers but no <u>friends</u>, all mere <u>outsiders</u>. There is a charming old gentleman of whom I am becoming very fond, Gen. Martin.[139] I have made an agreement with him to practise an hour every day. He has but one arm having lost the other in Mexico and he is altogether quite a veteran. Last evening we spent with Mrs. James Anderson, a great friend of Della's.

11 April 1864
Chicora Wood

My darling Brother,

 I tremble at the thought of how much you will suffer when you read the sad contents of this letter. It is hard to have to write it. We have no longer a father on Earth. Our beloved Papa has left us. Last Thursday (7th) afternoon at four o'clock his sufferings ended. It is very terrible. It seems strange that we can live on after such a loss, but the place looks as peaceful, the birds sing as charmingly and the sun shines as brightly as when he was here to enjoy it all. Oh brother how we longed for you during the two weeks of his illness. We wanted your strength to raise him and help him when he was so weak. Not even Charley was with us, nor Cousin Joe, and poor Will was and is too ill to leave his house.[140] He did all he could and sent John to help nurse Papa.

 I must go back several weeks and try and tell you all I remember about it. You know the months I spent with Della in Wilmington. Those two months Mamma spent with Papa down here, part of the time in Plantersville, and when it became so cold they moved a very few

---

[139] General James Green Martin (1819-1878) of North Carolina was a veteran of the Mexican American War. He was the commander-in-chief of his state's military forces and later went into field service in Virginia.

[140] Will was William Allan Allston (1834-1878). A nephew of Bessie's father Robert F.W. Allston, he was a rice planter who lived at Woodville Plantation on Pawley's Island. In *Chronicles of Chicora Wood*, Bessie recorded that he sent over "a very faithful man named John Locust" to be of help.

1864

things and stayed here. When they returned to Croley I joined them from Wilmington on Thursday 17th March. The next day, Friday, Papa left us to go to Georgetown on business for a few days and said he would return to us the next Saturday. All that week the weather was dreadful. Monday and Tuesday it snowed and sleeted by turns all day and the snow remained on the ground three days. Mamma and I felt rather lonely by ourselves and looked forward with longing to Saturday and his return. The next day was Easter Sunday and we were hoping for good weather that we might go to church. Saturday morning at about seven o'clock we were startled by the arrival of Quash from home. He brought a note from Mr. Belflowers to Mamma saying that Papa was "quite sick" and that "Dr. Sparkman thought it necessary that some of his family should be with him."[141] Nothing more, no particulars. We got ready immediately and were on the road by half past nine.

That night we went to Mrs. Fryers about half way and next morning we started at dawn, [met] the horses at Union church and reached here at about five in the afternoon. We went up to see Papa and felt much pleased and relieved not to find so ill [sic] as we had feared. He was perfectly natural and did not seem very weak tho' his breath was cut short by a sort of gasp constantly. He was very affectionate but tho' he seemed glad to see us was very angry with Mr. Belflowers and Dr. Sparkman for having summoned us to him without consulting him. He said he had given Mr. Belflowers a talk about it.

We brought quite a packet of letters for him from Croley, and he said that I must read them to him, which I did that night and the next morning, and he

---

141   Jesse Belflowers was Mr. Allston's trusted overseer; he died in 1866 and is buried in Prince Frederick's churchyard. Quash was likely a slave sent from Chicora Wood Plantation. Dr. Sparkman was James Ritchie Sparkman (1815-1897), a physician and planter.

dictated the answers to some of the most important while I wrote them. He was very cheerful and spoke of going to Columbia the middle of April or the first of May. The night we came he inquired anxiously "Where is Jane?" He thought that she had come home for Easter and was anxious for her to remain with us, not to return to school at all.[142] When he found that she had not come he said "We must send for her." After that he never asked for anyone who was not present. Mamma and I felt very much more cheerful and hopeful. He was so much so, and he was so very patient and uncomplaining. We did not fully realize how much he suffered. The Doctor told us that when he sent for us he had scarcely hoped we would arrive in time, but Papa did not think himself so ill and our faith in his judgment was stronger than in that of the Doctor.

Monday night however he had a horrible attack of gasping and we all thought him dying. He thought so himself for the first time. He told us Goodbye and gave some directions as well as he could with the difficulty of breathing, but the attack passed and the next morning, he seemed better. Then we fondly hoped that the crisis was past but the Doctor never varied or gave us hope of his recovery for an instant. So that day I wrote to Della and Jane to come at once, also to Charley. Della, Arnoldus and Jane arrived Saturday night at one o'clock. Since Tuesday until that time he had not seemed worse tho' he was weaker. The Doctor said that he might remain in that condition for weeks or that it might terminate very suddenly. He treated him with the greatest attention and devotion. He always spent the night here and all day, with the exception of a very few hours. Mr. John LaBruce was very kind.[143] He sat up

---

142 Bessie's sister Jane (Jinty) was at Madame Togno's school at Barhamville.
143 John LaBruce (1820-1877) was a Georgetown District rice planter, and the brother of Joshua Ward LaBruce.

1864

Tuesday, Thursday and Saturday nights of that week and Monday of the next. Mr. Weston sat up one night but he seemed to annoy Papa and besides it knocked him up. Mamma or myself was always in the room tho' never mind who sat up.

It was a comfort to see Della, Arnoldus and Jane arrive. We had not told Papa that they had been sent for and we did not tell him at all. The next day Della went into the room while he was asleep and sat by the bed and fanned him, so that as soon as he woke he saw her. He did not seem at all excited or surprised, simply extended his hand to her. Jane was in and out of the room two days before he noticed her at all, then he pressed her hand without a word. His mind was perfectly clear and he was as thoughtful and considerate as ever.

Tuesday morning he had a very bad turn and as soon as it had passed he sent for Mr. Belflowers and gave him directions as to who should make the coffin. He expressed a wish to be laid in the enclosure at the church where Mr. J. H. Allston is buried. Mr. Glennie came that morning and had prayers.[144] We were all in the room. Papa was perfectly calm and resigned. His constant prayer was for "Patience" and certainly it was granted to him for he never showed the smallest irritation or impatience tho' his sufferings were intense and his speech was so broken that it was almost impossible to understand him, so that often we must have annoyed him very much by misunderstanding his wishes, but he never showed it.

When he became too weak to help himself it was so difficult to move him comfortably. John was not very strong. After Stephen came he helped but it was not enough and I fear he must often have suffered from it. It is a terribly painful thought to us but it was impossible

---

144 This was Alexander Glennie (1804-1880), an Episcopal minister.

to have it otherwise. Cousin Joe was anxious to come but he was just under orders for Fort Sumter and that of course made it impossible. Tuesday Dr. Sparkman took a very bad cold and was quite sick and had to go home that night. Frank Heriot came over to sit up, so he and Mamma, Della and Arnoldus all sat up by turns.[145]

Wednesday morning he was much more comfortable. When Mr. Glennie came he said to him "Yesterday you did not expect to see me alive today." Mr. Glennie said no he had not. Then Papa said "It is harder to live than to die now, but I am willing to live if it is God's will and I'm not afraid to die." He spoke at long intervals and we were obliged to listen attentively for every word. During that day I was sitting by him fanning him and someone else was in the room too. He said: "Oh my beloved, if God would but give me strength to talk to you!" But that was not granted. It would have been an inexpressible comfort to us to know his wishes and last thoughts. Wednesday evening he seemed still more easy. We persuaded Mamma to lie down. She had been up all the day and night before.

We expected Mr. LaBruce to sit up that night but he did not come, so that Stephen, Caroline and I were his only attendants.[146] I promised to call Mamma at five in the morning. Until twelve Papa was very restless and did not sleep at all. About half past twelve he went to sleep and slept until just half past one, when he woke in great suffering. I offered him gruel, but he shook his head and said "I'm dying" and his feet and hands were very cold. I rubbed them with mustard and then ran and called Mamma as he said

---

145 Frank Heriot was probably Francis Withers Heriot (1825-1873), whose home was Mount Arena Plantation on Sandy Island.

146 This was Joshua Ward LaBruce (1823-1887) of Sandy Island. Stephen was likely Stephen Gallant, whom Bessie described in *Chronicles* as "papa's special servant and valet." Bessie also mentioned a family maid named Caroline.

"Call them." The agony lasted until sunrise, when he became quiet, but he was bathed in a cold sweat all the morning and was very much exhausted, but slept quite frequently for a short space.

The Doctor came and stayed a few minutes and left quite ill. After he had gone Papa asked for him. Mr. Glennie came and prayed with him. Frank Heriot and Arnoldus were here. The Doctor ordered that the blister over his chest and heart should be dressed and Mamma had to do it. She shrank from giving him so much pain but she had to do it. He did not groan tho' it must have been terrible in his exhausted condition. He only gasped out the word "torture." Cousin Lizzie was here, he spoke to her and blessed herself and children.[147]

As we stood around the bed he looked at us and said "God will provide when I am gone." Some moments afterwards he turned on his side and asked for gruel which we gave him and offered him some brandy, but he refused to take [that]. The difficulty in his breathing was so great that tho' it was a cool day, two of us were fanning him and motioned to Mamma to put up the window. I never heard anything like the birds. They seemed so near, they must have been on the shed. I think he heard them with pleasure tho' he said nothing, for when someone went to close the window he shook his head.

Suddenly his breathing became more difficult. He murmured "Lord let me pass" closed his eyes and soon all was still. We could not believe that his spirit had flown. We chafed his hands and feet, but in vain. It was long before warmth left his heart, but Mr. Belflowers, Mr. Heriot and Arnoldus came and we were forced to believe the overwhelming truth, that he was gone from

---

147 Cousin Lizzie was Elizabeth Blyth Tucker Weston, the daughter of Bessie's Aunt Elizabeth Ann Allston Tucker (1790-1822). Her husband was Francis Weston (1811-1890).

us. Oh brother it is very terrible to be left all alone. All alone as we are, it is too terrible to think that we will never see his strong manly face again with its kindly affectionate look. He was wonderfully beautiful all day Friday as he lay so calm, so majestic. A happy smile settled on his features and he looked so much younger, just as I remember him when I was a little child long ago.

Poor Charley did not reach here in time to take a last look at his beloved face. Frank Heriot and Arnoldus made all the arrangements for the funeral to take place Friday afternoon at five. We could not bear it to be so soon but did not interfere. All day we hoped Charley would come. We wanted him so to see Dear Papa once again and to have the beautiful impression of him left on his mind and oh my darling brother if you only could have been here, it would have been such a comfort.

Arnoldus was devotedly kind and thoughtful but we wanted you so much. Papa [asked] Dr. Sparkman to write a codicil for him appointing Mr. Robertson an executor as you were not here.[148] He told us to write Uncle Henry as soon as all was over and ask him to come. Brother I can't write anymore. Mamma is wonderfully supported in this sore affliction. She is very calm. It was pitiful to see the people as they came in one by one to take a last farewell of him who was so much to them. They followed him to his last resting place with respectful and solemn silence.

Goodbye my dearest. Give my warmest love to sister Ellen.[149] I feel very sad that she will never know the kind fatherly love he would have tendered her. As

---

148 Alexander Robertson (1804-1888), of the firm of Robertson, Blacklock and Company, was Mr. Allston's factor in Charleston.

149 This was Bessie's new sister-in-law Ellen Stanley Robinson (1841-1875), whom her brother Benjamin Allston met in Texas during his military service. In 1863, Benjamin Allston was transferred to the Trans-Mississippi Department of the Confederate Army, becoming inspector general for General Edmund Kirby Smith. He and Ellen were married on February 24, 1864.

1864

soon as he read your letter two months ago he said to Mamma "Write to him to send her home and we will take care of her." Goodbye again and earnest love to you both.

Your devoted sister, Bessie

In *Chronicles,* Bessie described how her father's remains were to be taken to the burial place at the church of Prince Frederick's Parish. She resumed her diary after her return to Croly Hill with her grieving mother.

He was laid to rest in the churchyard of Prince Frederick's, just a mile away, where the beautiful half-finished brick church in whose building he had been so much interested, stood, a monument to war. All the trimmings and furnishings had been ordered in England, and, in running the blockade, they had been sunk. The architect, whose name was Gunn, had died, and was buried near the church, and the roofless but beautiful building stood there forlorn. There we laid him, with all the beauty of the wild spring flowers and growth he loved around him, nearly under a big dogwood-tree in all its white glory.

Diary

May 20th 1864. Wednesday evening we got back here after an absence of nearly two months and oh what an age it seems.[150] What desolation has fallen upon us. It is so strange that we should live on now that Papa our strength in everything is gone, now that we have to live only in the remembrance of his kind unwearying love! Oh it is hard, so very hard, to be left all alone. My darling papa, to think of his familiar, noble, kindly face lying in that quiet grave all by himself. While we

---

150 Bessie and her mother and sister returned to Croly Hill.

were at G[eorgetown] we went every now and then and laid fresh flowers on his bed—the lovely roses he loved so well, but he wished us to come back here.[151] He said so during his illness and of course all that remains to us of his wishes we are eager to carry out. Oh I tremble with fear that his image may be taken from me, that I may lose the remembrance of his calm earnest hope of salvation, that I may cease to strive to live so that I may one day join him in that "home of the soul" where the wicked cease from troubling and the weary are at rest. It is hard to realize that in the little trials of everyday life we must be guarded by that same hope, and I am so weak. Oh, that I were strong—strong to yield, strong to obey, strong to keep down that unruly monster the tongue, strong to comfort and assist poor Mamma, and above all strong to conquer myself, to conquer that proud, rebellious, impetuous self that is always ready to oppose any and everyone. God Almighty give me the strength of a meek heart and trusting, humble spirit.

Life looks to me very dreary and hopeless now and yet I know that my mission is to comfort and support Mamma, as much as for me lies henceforth to devote my life to her, and as far as I can help Jane forward by showing her my steadfast love, and tho' I feel that I am able to see thus far I am so incompetent for even that duty, so utterly unworthy and miserable that I fear I am much more of a trouble than a comfort to dear Mamma. And yet I know and feel that I have something nobler and better in me—if by one great sacrifice I could add to Mamma's happiness I would willingly, gladly do it, and yet in <u>little things</u> it is so hard to yield without showing a temper. I know it is because I don't struggle as I should against [sic]. When I remember the

---

151   Robert F.W. Allston was initially buried at the church of Prince Frederick's Parish, and soon afterward, reinterred in the graveyard of Prince George Winyah Episcopal Church in Georgetown.

1864

many many times I have grieved the best and kindest of fathers by my wayward willful ways now remorse and unavailing regret overpowers me, and I feel that I can now best please him and atone in some way for my past carelessness and negligence to him, by devoting my whole life to Mamma as long as she needs me. Oh may he look down and help me with his presence.

27 June 1864
Croley

Dearest Brother,

I got your letter of May [18th] two or three days ago. I was distressed that you had not received my letter of April 9th or 10th telling of dear Papa's illness and death. I suppose of course you will have got it before this reaches you and you will understand how desolate and changed everything is to us now. Mamma wrote to you at the same time. She sent hers by way of [Mobile] and I sent mine to [Custis Lee] in Richmond who offered Della to forward letters to you. Charley was at home on two weeks holiday when your letter arrived. He has not been very well this spring. When he came down to Chicora in April, he was quite sick, suffering from his [illegible word or words]. He seems entirely well again now. He left us Wednesday to return to Willington. Cousin Min lives at the Harris place [very near] Mr. Porcher's and Charley by her request stays with her instead of [illegible word] at school. He likes the arrangement very well tho' it has its drawbacks.

Cousin Joe is at home now [having] been wounded in the ankle at Petersburg.[152] The wound is by no means dangerous but painful and this keeps him at home a long time, that is two or three months. Charley

---

152 Bessie's cousin Joseph Blyth Allston (1833-1904).

Porcher who is now 2nd Lieut. of the company was also wounded in the fight. He has not yet left the hospital in Richmond. His wound is in the leg and his condition tho' painful is not dangerous. The number of our wounded is terrible. I heard yesterday that Major Pinckney Alston was hopelessly ill, his right arm amputated, a wound in the side and one in the leg.[153] I know so little of how much you know of them. I suppose you have seen in the papers if you ever get any how Rutledge's regiment was hurried forward fighting as infantry before Richmond. How gloriously they fought and how terrific the slaughter was.[154] I heard two days ago that there were but three members of the Charleston Light Dragoons left. Of course that might be a mistake but the loss has been immense. Poor Aleck Robertson and Mr. Kirkland were killed.[155] Great numbers were captured and many [can't] be heard of at all. Among the latter poor Frank Middleton, Phil's friend.[156] You would be surprised to hear how much Aunt Lou and the girls hope. They live in constant expectation of hearing news of Phil either as a prisoner picked up by some of the Yankee soldiers or by some vessel bound for some distant port. Outside of the immediate family no one feels the slightest hope that the crew of the "Juno," will be heard from. You know two such men were saved, one of them came in to Wilmington. Arnoldus saw [him] and inquired for the particulars. He said Phil was in one of the lifeboats (of which there were two just large enough to hold the crew) fully manned and provisioned but the

---

153 Thomas Pinckney Alston was wounded in the Battle of Jericho Ford (Virginia) in May 1864 and died on June 19, 1864.

154 Bessie is referring the Battle of Haw's Shop, fought on May 28, 1864, in Virginia, in which almost half of the Charleston Light Dragoons were killed. The Dragoons were Company K in the 4th South Carolina Cavalry Regiment, which was commanded by Colonel Benjamin H. Rutledge (1828-1893).

155 Private Alexander Robertson (1840-1864), and William Lennox Kirkland (1828-1864).

156 Francis Kinloch Middleton (1835-1864) was mortally wounded at Haw's Shop and died on May 30, 1864.

1864

smokestack of the steamer fell across it and capsized it. Of course that almost puts an end to hope.[157]

The poor Vanderhorsts are in great trouble. John died the other day at Aiken after three days illness and Louis is among the missing in the Dragoons.[158] It is reported that he was seen to fall, shot through the head, but his body has not been found and they hope he may be only captured. Aunt Louise took a house in Charleston so as to be near Phil and Charley, who was then on the coast but now neither of them are there and they feel very lonely in a little house in Mary St. The shells come nearer to them every day and I should not be surprised if they had to leave before the summer is over on that account.[159]

Mamma is thinking seriously of spending the summer at the place in No[rth] Carolina. We will certainly be there a month at the least. The account of all the crops are bad. The rice has been almost floated away by the excessive rains and the [replant] crop has suffered also. I hope however things will improve. It is very hot and dry now. Things go on better than we had reason to expect and I hope they will continue so. Uncle Henry's health is still miserable, so much so as almost to incapacitate him for any active business. He spends his time on the R.R. going from Charleston to Spartanburg and back. Of course such a life does not improve his health. If he could place his family nearer to Charleston where all his business lies it would be very much better. He

---

157 Bessie's cousin, Lt. Philip Johnstone Porcher, Jr., was in command of the *Juno* (renamed the *Helen*), a steamship that served as a blockade runner and a torpedo boat. After sailing out of Charleston harbor on March 9, 1864, the ship encountered stormy weather and sprang a leak. When the ship broke in two, the crew escaped in lifeboats, but Porcher's lifeboat capsized.

158 John Vanderhorst (1832-1864), the brother of Arnoldus Vanderhorst, died on June 14, 1864.

159 Beginning in August 1863, the city of Charleston was under bombardment from Morris Island, which was soon entirely under enemy control by September. This bombardment became the longest siege of the war.

has sold his house in Charleston and leased this farm in Spartanburg for two years. He has an office in Columbia also but never stops there more than a day or two. Mr. Robertson's health is also failing and I fear the death of his son will make it worse.[160]

Everyone is very kind to us. Mr. W[ilia]m Evans our very near neighbor has been devotedly kind in assisting Mamma with advice and in many other ways.[161] John Williams has made many offers, that is asked to be called upon if he could be any assistance, but the truth is he has a good deal to occupy him in attending to his own and his mother's affairs and his aid has not gone beyond offers. I think it is good for Mamma to have the business to attend to. It keeps her mind occupied and prevents her dwelling on our sorrow. She is wonderfully cheerful, and tho' the business is very worrying sometimes, on the whole it is better than for her to give it into the hands of the other executors who both seem ailing.

Dear Brother, Mamma and all of us think it best that you should not try to come over now. It might injure you some to apply either for a leave or transfer at this time, therefore tho' nothing could possibly give us so much pleasure as the thought of seeing you soon we understand and feel that for the present you cannot possibly change your position. I hope you will make no effort that could in the remotest way compromise your reputation. I know you will understand what I mean.

I got a letter from Della day before yesterday. She was quite well and my dear brother you need not be anxious about her. I think she is as happy as she could

---

160   Alexander Robertson (1804-1888) was Robert F. W. Allston's factor in Charleston. His son was Alexander Robertson (1840-1864).

161   This was William Henry Evans (1819-1892), who is buried in Society Hill. His plantation was called Pine Top. He had a son named John Witherspoon Evans (1844-1915).

1864

be under existing circumstances. Arnoldus is a kind and devoted husband and is anxious to be a son to Mamma—a real relative to us all. His presence was a comfort in our first hour of desolation and we would have felt much more intensely our loneliness without him, and he was as kind and gentle as a woman in helping nurse Papa. Of course such recollections have made a stronger tie between us than could ever have existed otherwise. He is mortal, and no mortal is faultless. He is devoted to Gen. Whiting and I'm sorry to say that the reports of Gen. W's conduct at Petersburg has been such to cause all his friends much pain. I don't for a moment believe them to be true but it will take some great [exploit] on his part to undo the damage done by them. It is certain that he did not execute an important order given to him by Gen. Beauregard. Everyone says he was incapable of carrying it out because of his old infirmity. You can imagine what indignation is felt and how rapidly the report spread and how eagerly people accepted it as true. I feel very much for the Gen. He is perfectly temperate now. It only shows how impossible almost it is for one to rid themselves [sic] of such a stain on his name and character. He is a very charming person. I liked him very much while we were in Wilmington.[162]

I'm afraid you can't read what I've written but Charley's letter must go in the same envelope so I must cross or not say what I want but I will stop now.[163] Give my most affectionate love to Ellen. We long to see both of you. Mamma and Jane send love.

Your affectionate sister, Bessie

---

162 In 1864, General William Henry Chase Whiting briefly served under General P.G.T. Beauregard in Virginia, and failed in an attempt to carry out part of Beauregard's strategy at Petersburg. It was rumored that Whiting was debilitated by drink, but it was more likely that his incapacity resulted from a lack of sleep.

163 Bessie is referring to cross writing, in which lines are written over others at right angles.

[P.S.] I have undertaken Jane's education for the present. It is quite amusing. Her will is so much the stronger that she has things much her own way. I will send this to Mr. McPherson.

Diary

June 28th 1864. Sunday 26th I was confirmed. I have often thought being [sic] confirmed before but never made up my mind altogether to it until this year. When I was at Wilmington I heard that the Bishop would be there soon and I thought of being confirmed then but I left before he came. I know I am utterly unworthy of the name and privileges of a Christian, but I trust that I may have grace granted me to improve daily and repent truly of all my sins.[164]

Sept. 6th 1864. This morning I got a nice long letter from Della, also one from Cousin Sue. The latter surprised me very much and I must say rather overwhelmed me for the time being. It was a kind letter tho' and I thank her for it. I have been owing Addy a letter for several months and must answer it soon. This summer has passed like a flash, tho' the days have been long enough. I have accomplished nothing in this time, <u>nothing</u>. I wonder that I can write it so cooly. I commenced teaching Jane but it did not succeed and I stopped. Mamma was not satisfied and undertook the English herself but it dropped through in a very short time so now Jane only reads a little history to Mamma every day. Then I began Macauley, but I have not yet accomplished the first volume! Voila une histoire honteuse![165] I wish I could get a governess of Jane [sic]. She would do better with me. I think she has an excellent mind, clear and bright.

---

164 Bessie was likely confirmed at Trinity Episcopal Church in Society Hill. The bishop of South Carolina at the time was Thomas Frederick Davis (1804-1871).

165 Translated, this means "Here is a shameful story."

1864

Well I believe my mind was once called clear and bright. It certainly has lost both qualities already and may now be described as dull and muddy. I shall make a full and free confession of my present state of mind to this faithful book and may hap seeing it on paper in my own hand-write [*sic*] may help me to amend it. Eh bien—I am frightfully morbid and much given to think that no one loves me and consequently that there is something hateful in me that nothing will ever overcome. Then come thoughts and doubts as to whether it would not be better for me to pass away and leave my place to be filled by better and more useful members. All this gives rise to a gloomy sullenness of manner that is enough I'm sure to make people detest me; or else a carping, ironical fiend takes possession and grins and shouts until Mama is nearly distracted. This however doesn't last always but gives place to a dreary, laughing sort of nonchalance as to affairs in general, which people take for cheerfulness and contentment which in reality is something approaching imbecility, and my time passes between morbid, wicked longings and selfish indifference to things around. It is only rarely I feel the buoyant joyful sense of pleasure that I used to have; it used to come when I looked out at a bright sky, or beautiful flower. There was a thankful sense of the beauty and excellence of life and an aspiration to be in harmony with all the beautiful and useful works of God. Now I feel often weary and wonder if I shall ever feel otherwise—if I shall ever be of use in the world, or if I am always to be the same cipher, the same useless nonentity. Oh forbid. There are many ways in which I might do good and be useful, but I have such a miserably awkward way of commencing, that all my efforts for good terminate in just the wrong direction. I once remember hearing a little boy repeat in the most reluctant and lugubrious manner, "try, try, try again." I'm afraid I must repeat like the little boy without putting my heart into it. There is no use writing now. I shall try to chronicle some improvement from day to day. It is truly <u>now</u> or <u>never</u>.

Friday Sept. 23rd. Today has been quietly happy to me. I had a loving letter from Ruth, then we went to church and had a very solemn service; after we came home Lynch Pringle came to see Mamma.[166] I gave Jane holiday and this evening we went to ride together behind the carriage, which contained Mamma and Mrs. Evans. At the depot I had a very pleasant chat with Rebecca P.[167] She tells me that Sabina Lowndes is engaged to Dr. Wm. Huger, a mutual [case] of consolation, he for Miss Sue, she for a Capt. Myers.[168] Well I hope she will be happy. After tea I commenced reading aloud "The Marble Faun." Something led to it and Mama told us all about my little sister Fanny's death.[169] It is very sad and must have been a terrible trial to Mama. She was two and a half years older than Della. Now I must go to bed thanking God for his goodness today.

Thursday Sept. 29th/64. This afternoon at four we returned from No. Ca. with the hope and expectation of seeing Aunt Lou and the girls tonight. But among the letters here was one from Aunt L saying Marianna was quite sick with "Neck fever" and they cannot think of coming now.[170] We are sadly disappointed and distressed at the cause. A letter from Jim Carson. He is in Fort Sumter for

---

166 This was Dominic Lynch Pringle (1846-1919), a younger brother of John Julius Pringle.

167 This was Rebecca Brewton Pringle (1839-1905), the daughter of Mary Motte Alston Pringle, matriarch of a large, wealthy family of Charleston. After the war Rebecca married Francis LeJau Frost (1837-1912). During much of the war Rebecca and others in her family lived near Society Hill.

168 Dr. William Harleston Huger (1826-1906) of Charleston married Sabina Lowndes (1840-1921), the daughter of Charles Tidyman Lowndes, on May 12, 1866.

169 In 1837, Mrs. Allston gave birth to a daughter named Charlotte Francis Allston, who died in June 1843.

170 Also known as "stiff-neck fever" this was probably a type of meningitis.

1864

20 days. I hope nothing will happen him [sic]. A [sweet] letter from Della. Julius Pringle left her on the 27th for Va. He spent a day and night with them. We left Morven at eight, all wishing to stay longer, but the thought of seeing [Min] and Annie reconciled, Jane and she coming to town and now can't bear to go back. While there I have been reading the Country Parson diligently and admire and love it very much.[171] Things on the farm progress badly. But the people seem generally cheerful and content. The molasses making is a great source of interest to all. Coming down I commenced a sock and knit over an inch on it. Mrs. Evans came over after tea. It must be near twelve so to be with warm thanks.

Oct. 1st 1864. Last night Aunt Louise, Uncle Phil, Annie and Min arrived, after passing thro' numerous perils of shell and fever.[172] It is delightful to have them. They all look badly, Annie especially. Yesterday Hagaar brought me the things sent by Acelie in leaving—Ellen's desk and her little garnet bracelet and several books of her own. Madame sent me her book of French ballads and Acelie her "Trovatore and Traviata" bound together.

Oct. 2nd 1864. I am just going to bed but I must write a few lines. I have spent a quiet day. It was Communion Sunday, which must always make one feel more vividly the interest and love of God towards us. I wrote a long letter to Ruth today.

Oct. 3rd. This morning is rainy and gloomy looking in the extreme. It makes one feel low-spirited and rather cross. Annie is still suffering very much—I think is in a distressing state, entirely depressed. She sits all day in an armchair without moving her position. I think it

---

171   *The Country Parson* was the only prose work of George Herbert (1593-1633), an English poet and Anglican priest.

172   Uncle Phil was Philip Johnstone Porcher, and Aunt Louise, his wife. Annie and Min are possibly their daughters Mary Anna Porcher (1840-1875), whom Bessie earlier referred to as Marianna, and Marion Porcher (1848-1907), whom Bessie earlier called "Little Min."

is her silent grief and agony that is weighing her down so. I would give a great deal to be able to cheer or comfort her ever so little, but she seems as hard as stone as far as the receiving of signs of affection and love go. Her heart seems locked against the present, filled only with the Past. I have been trying to get Jane to study her lessons today, but she has thus far positively refused. "I will not" is her unvariable answer. Min is very lovely. I think she is beautiful, and she is apparently unconscious of it.

Mamma told me two days ago to write to Miss Manigault and ask her if she would take Jane as a boarder.[173] I have not done it yet. This morning I commenced reading Prescot's History of the Conquest of Mexico. I read aloud to Minnie as she had some sewing to do and she is to read when I have any work on hand. I wrote the note to Miss M[anigault] but Mama did not like it, so she wrote herself which was much better.

Oct. 4th 1864. No letter from Ruth today tho' I hoped for one very much. Annie got a letter from Della mentioning the funeral of Mrs. Rose Greenhow [who] was drowned while running the blockade.[174] It seems very sad after all the trials she endured at the North on account of her Southern feelings. I am reading Gen. Jamieson's "Bertrand Du Guesclin." I have thus far found it very interesting.[175] I must finish it soon. It is Aunt Lou's book. Poor Gen Jamieson died of Yellow Fever in Charleston

---

173   This was likely Ann Julia Horry Manigault (1829-1890). As early as October 1862, she was operating a school in Columbia, S.C., and was likely still there in 1864. In 1865 she and her sister Emma established a boarding and day school in Yorkville, S.C. By 1874, Julia Manigault was operating a school in London, Ontario.

174   Rose O'Neal Greenhow (1813-1864), a Confederate spy, was drowned near Wilmington, North Carolina, after running the blockade to return from a diplomatic mission in Europe.

175   David Flavel Jamison was at this time the presiding judge for the military court of General Beauregard's command. He was the author of *The Life and Times of Bertand Du Gueselin: A History of the Fourteenth Century*, which was printed in England and brought into the Confederacy through the blockade. Jamison died of yellow fever on September 14, 1864.

the other day. Jim is in Fort Sumter. I truly hope he may escape and Hall too. They say he is in a sad state of mind.

Oct. 5 Wednesday. This morning Mamma got a letter from Della. It was short and hurried and Mamma has taken the idea that she is sick. I hope it may not be so. Mama wrote to A to say she thought he ought to send Della home as there is a very malignant and mysterious fever down at Smithville.[176] Doctors are entirely at a loss how to treat it. Recovery is hopeless when it attacks its victim. Annie looks much better and is much more herself, but she has an air of constraint that I cannot account for or understand. I wish it was gone. I can't feel comfortable with her because of it and I really am fond of her. I suppose she finds me too silly to talk to.

Jane said her lessons with no difficulty today, early and well. I only read 50 pages of Mexico. Min doesn't seem to like it much. "Bertand" is beautifully printed and done up. It is a pleasure to handle such an elegant looking volume. Miss Evans sent over some flowers to "the sick lady" who appeared much satisfied. The news yesterday and today has not been good. There have been reverses in Va and many of our cavalry killed. Della mentions that Capt Pembroke Jones of the Navy is staying with them.[177]

Thursday Oct 6th. This morning Jane and I went at Mama's request to the Distillery with the wagon. It is 10 miles or more. The whiskey which Mama has ordered for the plantation was not done so it was a bootless errand. Got a letter from dear little Sara this morning saying she supposed I did not receive her last which I

---

176 Smithville, North Carolina, is now called Southport. The "mysterious fever" was likely yellow fever.

177 John Pembroke Jones (1825- 1910) was a Confederate naval officer whose commands included the ironclad *North Carolina*.

am ashamed to say I never answered. Mama this evening talked much.

Oct 7th. Aunt Lou in bed today. A short letter from Ruth. Charlie arrived last night, school having broken up, Porcher's school.[178] He came up from the depot and slept in the [shedroom] us knowing nothing of it, until this morning. He looks well, rather thin. Mama has been in low spirits all day.

Oct. 9th Sunday. Last night I felt too bad to write. I was thinking of six months ago the 8th April we laid dear Papa in his lonely grave. It does seem so strange that everything goes on just the same and I wonder at our cheerfulness often, and now that Aunt Lou is here I wonder still more at theirs, for I think they are all more cheerful than we are. Min now looks very badly, but Mariana is looking very much better.

Yesterday Jane and Min dined with the Sam Evans.[179] They enjoyed themselves very much. This morning I got a sweet letter from Ruth. Her father is at home on a week's furlough and he says he is very hopeful about the cause. Ruth has been sick she says but is well again. There being no church today Mariana, Min, Jane, Charley and I took a long walk. The weather is charming, very clear and cold for the season. I think we must have walked more than five miles. Mariana is a charming companion. She was talking of her European trip. Her memory never fails her. I think she is almost the cleverest person I know. I wrote to Sara and Della yesterday. This morning a letter from Miss Julia Manigault saying she could not take a boarder.

---

178 Octavius T. Porcher's school near Willington continued until boys as young as sixteen were called into Confederate service in South Carolina. The remaining boys of that age and older in his school enlisted in reserve companies, and Mr. Porcher also entered military service.

179 This was likely the family of Samuel Wilds Evans (1823-1894), who was the brother of William Henry Evans.

1864

Oct. 10. I have just broken the crystal to Papa's watch. Oh I am so distressed. He had it so long and spoke of it several times as being such a good one, and I to think that I should break it.

Oct. 11th. This morning came a letter from Arnoldus saying Della would be home on Thursday. It will be delightful. Tonight Annie talked much about music and operas. I enjoyed it so much and sang several songs. I have promised Aunt Lou to take care of my complexion. I must try and keep it.

Oct. 12th. A telegram from Arnoldus from Richmond saying Della's visit would be postponed, so Mariana determined to start immediately for North Carolina. Mr. Evans went also. Charley, Jane, Sam and [Britby] formed her escort. I hope they have arrived safely. I am housekeeper and much impressed with the responsibility of that office.

Oct. 13th. No letter from Della today. Mariana is still in No Ca. Spent the evening with Mrs. E[vans]. Mr. E elected.[180]

Oct. 17th. Friday there came a letter from Della and a telegram saying she would be at Florence that night and asking that someone should meet her there. Charley being away and Della having been sick I determined to go down myself with Nelson, so off we started. That evening Mr. Stockton, Col Finney went down that afternoon also, but Constance did not think fit to introduce them, so the slight comfort their presence might have afforded was denied me.[181] At Florence the train remained about half an hour before the arrival of the Wilmington train. During that time I sat in the car

---

180 William Henry Evans served in the South Carolina legislature.
181 Colonel Finney was likely William Wood Finney (1829-1910), a native of Virginia. In February 1865 he married Constance Williams (1841-1916), the daughter of John Nicholas Williams (1797-1861) of Society Hill, S.C.

quite alone, Mr. Stockton sleeping soundly on the seat before me. There were several rowdy looking men who walked up and down the car and looked very impatient. At last one spoke to me. I was frightened. I did not hear his words but I know I did not show my fright. I looked steadily at him for an instant then turned my head away. He shrank off like an intimidated hound and left the car. A Louisiana soldier who had seen it all then came up and asked me to go to the hotel with him, but I declined then asked if he might take his seat by me to protect me from further inconvenience, but I told him I thought that unnecessary, and tho' he looked a perfect gentleman I did not care to be friendly with a perfect stranger. He very kindly took his stand beside me until the W[ilmington] train arrived and I found that he was a Captain of Engineers. He had been for four months in Fort Sumter and his health failing had been sent to Florence to build the stockade. He spoke very broken English. I did not find out his name for which I am very sorry. I shall ask Hal if he knows him.[182]

Della looks badly but seems to feel very well. When we got to the depot here the first person I saw was Mr. [R] Parker. He intended spending the night there so I asked him to come home and we would give him a bed and breakfast. He came and behaved very well. Saturday evening quite late the party from "Loch Adele" arrived, Mama with a bad cold, Charley driving.[183] Sunday we all went to church except Annie. Charley drove M, J and I in the spring wagon. Coming out of church Mrs. Pringle told me that she had a message for Mamma and me from Julius, which proved to be nothing more than his

---

182 This was probably Frederick Fraser Warley (1830-1876), whose rank was actually that of major. He was wounded and captured in Charleston harbor in September 1863, becoming a prisoner of war at Fort Delaware. The following year, in August 1864, he was exchanged and then assigned to build and command the stockade prisoner of war camp at Florence, S.C. His "broken English" might have been due to serious wounds he received in 1863.

183 Loch Adele was the Allston plantation near Morven, North Carolina.

1864

regards.[184] She told me also that Mrs. [Julius] had come through the lines.[185] Mrs. Evans tells me [he] had a narrow escape, with eight others, was surrounded by the enemy and reported dead for three days. I hope he may continue to escape for his poor Mother's sake.

Croley Hill
24 November 1864

Dearest Dell,

Mamma wrote you a few lines yesterday to tell of the sad fate of the blacks, poor things![186] I can't bear to think that the poor creatures have no future. They must have suffered so much too, plunging into a deep terrible stream without a moment's hesitation, so accustomed as they were to obey blindly, and trusting to man's superior intelligence. At first Mamma seemed to feel very bitterly towards Sam and Bri[tby] but tho' everyone allows it was great stupidity, there were many palliatory circumstances as neither had ever been on that road before and as Sam said they had gone through so much water he never thought of danger as that was the narrowest they had crossed.[187] Mr. Williams came to tell of the circumstances of yesterday. Even he says they drove off of a high bluff, higher than this room!! The freshet having risen and covered it all, they knew nothing of it until they plunged off the bluff into the depths of the water. It was a mercy they were not drowned also. Mamma feels the loss sadly. Until the horses come from

---

184   Mrs. Pringle was Jane Lynch Pringle (1811-1896), the mother of John Julius Pringle (1842-1876), Bessie's future husband.

185   "Mrs. Julius" was Maria Linton Duncan Pringle (1826-1908), the wife of John Julius Pringle (1824-1901). During much of the war she lived in Europe, but later returned to the United States. A family letter reported that in July 1864 she was in Newport, Rhode Island. Cote, *Mary's World*, 205.

186   Black horses.

187   Sam Maham and Britby (?) were Allston slaves.

below we will be without the means of hauling wood or anything else.

I went over this morning to talk it over with Mrs. Evans. She is busy preparing Dev to meet this call.[188] He leaves tomorrow to go to Hamburg. The news today is so dreadful. The enemy within 70 miles of Augusta and Milledgeville![189] I begin to feel almost as gloomy as Mamma and should like very much to ask Ruth to come to us, as I hear everyone is flocking from Georgia into Columbia, but Mamma does not second my proposal and it is very natural she should shrink from having a stranger in the house. I am perfectly certain Aunt Louise's visit did her much more harm than good. Indeed, I never saw Mamma so terribly depressed, overwhelmed almost, as after Aunt Louise's visit. I was really anxious for her mind. I force myself to think Aunt L. meant well, but certainly she was very much misguided in some of her notions of right and kindness! She succeeded in causing great suffering to all this household. Dear you know this page is meant only for your eyes and ear [sic]. Poor Mamma suffers a great deal. I wish I was more fit to soothe her suffering for I earnestly think that is all anyone could do.

I think it would be best after all for Jane to go to Mr. Caldwell, at least until something else is decided upon. She will there learn to study and be well grounded in English at least, which is very important. The school is conducted with such strict propriety and decorum that there will be little intercourse between the boys and herself. It is forbidden. She can't bear the idea of going because she is so very backward she is ashamed,

---

[188] Devonald D. Evans, who must have been about sixteen years old, was the son of William Henry Evans (1819-1892) and Jane Witherspoon Evans (1820-1897). He was leaving for Hamburg, South Carolina, to serve in the Junior Reserves, also known as the "Boy Brigade."

[189] During his infamous "March to the Sea" in 1864, General William T. Sherman burned a number of buildings in Milledgeville, the capital city of Georgia, including the railroad depot, factories, and storehouses containing Confederate government property.

1864

but she needs something to stimulate her ambition and nothing will do so more than going to that school. Anyway it is better for her to be doing <u>something</u> earnestly than nothing at all.

I don't know when Charley is coming up or whether he will have to go to Hamburg with the rest. Mrs. Evans says that he ought not to go as he is to enter the Arsenal and the appointment comes 1st December so that from that time he would be [liable] to duty with the Cadets.[190]

Col. [Finney] came this morning which was extremely polite of him and offered to carry a letter to you so I write by him. I think he is going to succeed.

There is a [illegible words] at Mr. Witherspoon's who sings beautifully.[191] I think they might bring him to see me as I have expressed my great desire to hear him sing. Miss Murdoch is enchanted with him. She has my book of French ballads and he comes over to sing with her every day. She says he has a beautiful Baritone voice and plays uncommonly well. He sings nothing but French.

I have made my merino dress with a little [illegible word] Cracovienne they call it. [Leonnie] cut and fit it for me and I made the body <u>myself</u>. It fits very well I think and so does Mamma. I believe I have told you all the news so I will say goodbye. Is [Anna] to be with you? I dreamt about her last night. Mamma and Jane send love.

Your sister

---

190   Bessie's brother Charles was sixteen years old. The Arsenal was the state military academy in Columbia, South Carolina.

191   This may have been the home of John Dick Witherspoon, Jr. (1818-1902).

This photograph of Elizabeth (Bessie) Waties Allston, circa 1860, was taken by the noted Charleston photographer George S. Cook. From the collections of the S.C. Historical Society.

Engraving of Bessie's father, Robert F.W. Allston (1801-1864).
From the collections of the S.C. Historical Society.

Adele Petigru Allston, later Mrs. Arnoldus Vanderhorst, circa 1860. From the collections of the S.C. Historical Society.

Bessie's mother, Adele Petigru Allston (1810-1896).
This is a photograph by Joseph Anderson of Charleston, circa 1880.
From the collections of the S.C. Historical Society.

This photograph of John Julius Pringle was likely made by George S. Cook of Charleston. The verso is inscribed "John Julus Pringle, Charleston Lt. Dragoons, Co. K, 4th S.C. Cav,, Society Hill, April 29th 1864." From the collections of the S.C. Historical Society.

Joel Roberts Poinsett Pringle (1843-1864), the younger brother of John Julius Pringle. From the collections of the S.C. Historical Society.

Twentieth century photograph of Chicora Wood Plantation on the Pee Dee River. Library of Congress.

John Julius Pringle, circa 1870.
From the collections of the S.C. Historical Society.

John Julius Pringle, circa 1875.
From the collections of the S.C. Historical Society.

Bessie in mourning, 1876. This photograph was taken by Frank A. Nowell of Charleston. From the collections of the S.C. Historical Society.

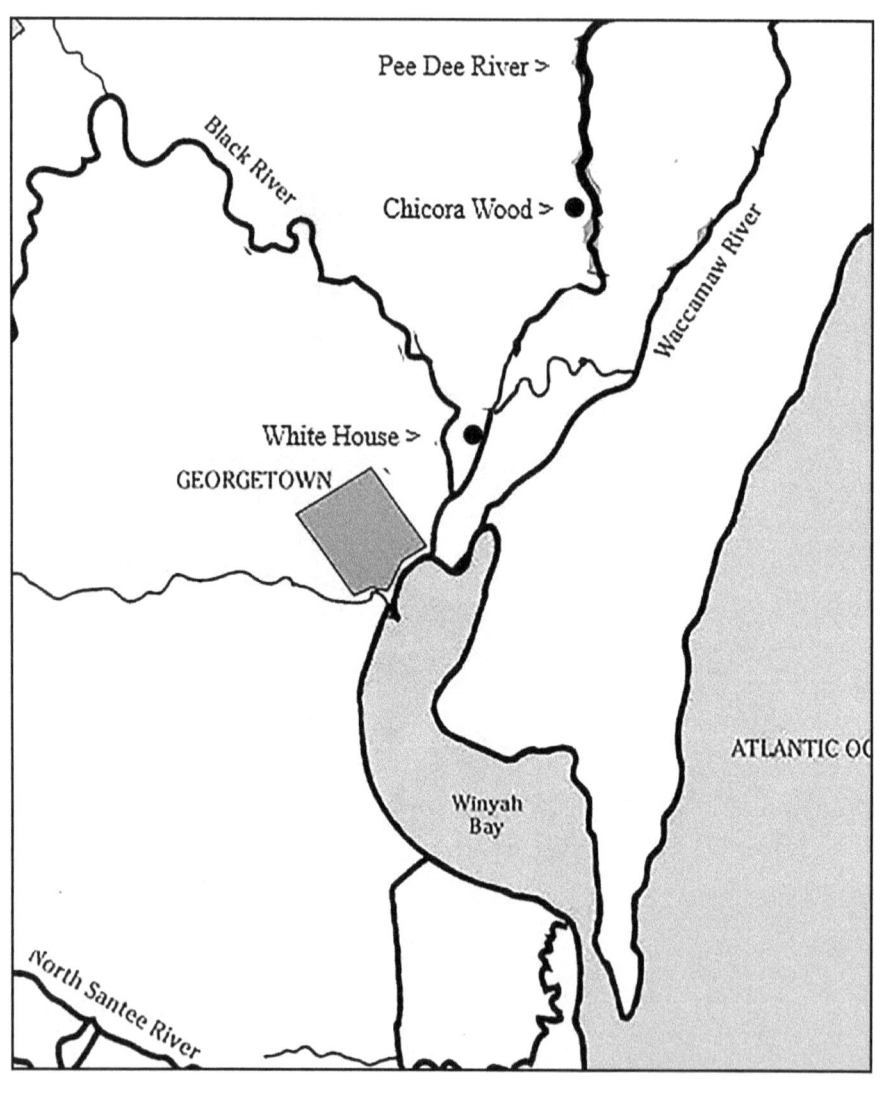

*Map of a portion of Georgetown County, South Carolina.
Based on a National Parks Service map adapted by the author.*

Map of South Carolina showing the location of Georgetown District.
Wikimedia Commons.

Miniature tintype of Bessie Pringle (ca. 1870?) produced by Wood's Gem Gallery in Albany, N.Y. From the collections of the S.C. Historical Society.

Chapter Five:

1865

IN THE LAST YEAR OF THE WAR, Bessie noted that things "were going worse and worse" for the Confederacy. The winter of 1865 was particularly traumatic for South Carolinians, as the state was invaded by a massive army of over 60,000 troops under the command of General William T. Sherman. He had completed his "March to the Sea" through Georgia by December 1864, and then turned his eyes toward the Palmetto State, beginning his main advance by February 1865. Sherman's stated intention, with which his soldiers cooperated with malevolent glee, was to "smash South Carolina all to pieces," and his campaign through the state was particularly brutal and destructive.[192] Moving across the counties from the coast into North Carolina, his soldiers burned farms, plantations, and towns, demolished railroads, destroyed or confiscated crops, farm implements, and livestock, and plundered and abused civilians. The worst barbarity of the march occurred when the state capital, Columbia—a city full of defenseless women, children, and old men—was surrendered by its mayor, only to be sacked and burned on February 17, 1865.

After leaving Columbia in ashes, Sherman's army moved on toward North Carolina, and a few of his regiments were sent into Darlington District, reaching Society Hill in early March. Bessie's friend Rebecca Pringle, whose residence was near Society Hill was visited by raiders, reported in a letter to her brother, "They robbed

---

192 Walters, *Merchant of Terror,* 184.

the negroes of everything, taking their shoes from their feet, and handkerchiefs from the women's heads...They have plundered everyone of everything most valuable."[193]

At Croly Hill, the Allstons were also visited by parties of enemy soldiers.

Diary

Jan. 21st 1865. A cold dreary rainy day! It keeps one shivering and shaking and huddling round the fire. Mamma thought of starting yesterday for the plantation, but fortunately she put it off until Monday. Since the fall of Wilmington everyone has been very gloomy. Della got a letter from Arnoldus saying through flag of truce they have heard that Gen. Whiting is doing very well. He fought with great gallantry as did Captain Van Benthuesen and his Marines.[194] Lt. Murdoch was taken prisoner also.

A few minutes ago Mrs. Evans sent a runner over with a piece of paper of good news. France and England are said to have recognized the Confederacy. So[uth] Ca[rolina] is to be defended, Johnston to come here and Lee's army to come to our assistance.[195] I don't think it can be true. We do need some good news so much. Things seem to get worse and worse but "hope on hope ever." I wrote to Addy King this morning. She is quite ill I hear through Annie who saw her lately. I sent a letter to Hal today and hope to get an answer. I read such a sad story in an old newspaper this morning, "Contesse Melisme." Strange how little things affect

---

193 This letter by Rebecca Pringle is found in the Alston-Pringle-Frost Papers at the South Carolina Historical Society.

194 Captain Alfred C. Van Benthuysen (died 1871), the commander of a detachment of marines, was seriously wounded in the defense of Fort Fisher near Wilmington in January 1865.

195 It was not true that France and England had officially recognized the Confederacy. General Robert E. Lee sent a small number of troops from Virginia to South Carolina in February, and General Joseph E. Johnston's army moved into North Carolina.

us! Mamma has the offer of Dr. Griffin's horses.[196] I don't know if they will suit her. We need a good pair very much.

Jan. 26th Chicora Wood. We arrived here almost frozen about six last evening. I never suffered from cold as I did on the ride down. Monday was a gloomy cloudy day but on the whole it was the pleasantest we had.

The Allstons returned to Croly Hill in February, and in *Chronicles,* Bessie recalled a poignant visit by John Julius Pringle, her future husband:

Things in the Confederacy were going worse and worse. It was an agony to read the papers. My sister, Mrs. Van der Horst, came home from Wilmington, bringing her maid, Margaret. Her husband did not think it safe for her to stay any longer there. It was a great comfort to have her with us. The Yankees were reported nearer and nearer, but we never saw any one to hear positively where they were. Then one evening, just at dusk, two horsemen galloped up to the front door, tied their horses and came in. They were Charleston Light Dragoons acting as scouts for General Wade Hampton—Julius Pringle and Tom Ferguson. They came to tell us Hampton was protecting all our troops as they left the State.[197] They were the very last, and Mr. Pringle said to mamma:

"I knew you had wine and whiskey in the house and I came to beg you for God's sake to destroy it all. Do not let a drop be found in the house, I implore you."

---

196   The horses were likely those of Dr. Peter Evans Griffin (1830-1904), a native of Society Hill.

197   In South Carolina, General Wade Hampton was moving his troops north, and the Confederate forces which had evacuated Charleston in mid-February were also marching up into North Carolina.

Mamma said: "But Julius, I have not sent all that whiskey to the hospitals yet, and it is so greatly needed! I have two demijohns still."

"Oh, Mrs. Allston, I implore you, do not hesitate. Have those demijohns broken to pieces the first thing to-morrow morning."

She promised. We gave them a good supper, of which they were in great need. Nelson fed the horses. They took two hours' sleep and then left in the middle of the night. As they were going, there were shots heard on the public road which ran back of our house about 400 yards. The two dragoons jumped on their horses and galloped off from the front door into the darkness of the night. It was an awful moment. They were gone, our last friends and protectors, and the agony in Mr. Pringle's face was indescribable.

Bessie wrote in *Chronicles* that her family anticipated the arrival of Sherman's soldiers by burying "every treasure we had." This included silverware, and barrels of "old Madeira" packed in a piano box. The women made bags to be worn under their skirts to conceal small valuables. Bessie's young brother Charles came to Croly Hill "on his way to Virginia, the boys at the Arsenal having been called out." He was sixteen years old, but he was a soldier now, and he left his family after a visit of a few days.

Finally, the day came when the enemy found Croly Hill.

As everything would be seized by the enemy when they came, we lived very high, and the things which had been preciously hoarded until the men of the family should come home were now eaten. Every day we had a real Christmas dinner; all the turkeys and hams were used. One day mamma had just helped us all to a delicious piece of turkey when Phibby rushed in, crying,"Miss, dey cumin!" Bruno, Jane's little water-spaniel, began to bark, and she rushed out to the wide

1865

roofless porch where he was, threw her arms around his neck and held his throat so tight he couldn't bark, just as a soldier was about to strike him with a sword. I was terrified for her as she knelt there in the middle of the porch, holding him, but they only looked down at her, as they rushed by on each side into the house, calling out:

"Whiskey! We want liquor! Don't lie; we know you have it! We want whiskey! We want firearms!" Each man said the same thing.

Mamma was very calm. As they clamored she said: "You may search the house. You will find none. I had some whiskey, but it is here no longer."

They seemed delighted at the sight of the dinner-table, and for a time were occupied eating and pocketing all that could be pocketed. When the renewed cry for wine, whiskey, and firearms came, mamma took from the nail where it hung the huge storeroom key, and went down the steps to the storeroom, just in time to prevent its being smashed in with an axe. She opened the door and they rushed in with many insulting words. Poor Phibby was wild with terror, and followed mamma, closely holding on to her skirt and entreating her not to go.

"Miss, dem'll kill yu, for Gawd sake don' go wid dem." But mamma showed no sign of excitement or alarm and never seemed to hear the dreadful things they said...

All this time there were parties going all over the yard, running ramrods into the ground to find buried things. My terror about that big box of wine was intense as I saw them. They even went under the big piazza at the back of the house and rammed every foot of the earth...As they left, Margaret and Nellie came in crying bitterly. They had taken every trinket and treasure they had, and all their warm clothes. Margaret was specially loud in her denunciation:

"I always bin hear dat de Yankees was gwine help de nigger! W'a' kind a help you call dis! Tek ebery ting I got in de world, my t'ree gold broach," etc., etc. Poor Margaret had sometimes been supposed to be light-fingered, and she had returned from Wilmington with a good deal of jewelry, which we wondered about: but now, poor soul, it was all gone. For four days the army kept passing along that road, and we heard shouts and shots and drums beating, and every moment expected another visit, but, as I said, they moved in haste, always fearing to leave the main road and be ambushed by Hampton's ubiquitous scouts.

Diary

March 1865. Twelve o'clock, and we still sit whispering over the fire, Phoebe on the floor nodding at the fire, Della with her feet extended trying to rest and I on a stool scribbling to while away the time until dawn. Thank God one more quiet day has passed and we so hoped for a quiet night, but a little after nine Phoebe ran in saying she heard them coming. We all knew well enough who <u>them</u> are. Oh the chill and terror that runs through me when I hear it. I always called myself a coward, but I never fully understood terror until now. And everyone says our experience of them was <u>mild</u>. They offered us no direct insult or injury but their mere presence is an insult. They are so low, so utterly devoid of honor and principle and so incapable of appreciating courage or spirit in man or woman. They delight in making terrible threats of vengeance before us and gloat over our misery.

Yesterday a captain was here who pretended to be all kindness and sympathy at the treatment we had

1865

received from the foragers. He was comparatively polite and did not enter the house. We placed a chair in the piazza and gave him what we had to eat, but when he began to talk he proved almost worst than any other. He vowed never to take a prisoner, said he would delight in cutting down a rebel prisoner and often did it. My disgust was intense but I struggled hard to keep cool and succeeded somewhat. He asked "Do you know what you are fighting for?" I replied "<u>Existence</u>." He said we won't let you have it with <u>such</u> a grin. I only said "<u>We'll see</u>." He said "in four months we'll have the Confederacy on its knees." When I replied "You must kill every man, woman and child first" he said "We'll do it too. At the beginning of this war I didn't care a cent about a nigger, but I'd rather enlist for ten years longer than let the South have her independence." Then with a chuckle he exclaimed "We'll starve you out, not one place that we have visited, have we left <u>three meals</u>." I laughed and said, "Pride goes before a fall we all know and in a short time I expect to hear of you fleeing in confusion to the coast, leaving guns, blankets and patriotism behind you!" "You'll never see us in such a fix," he replied. At something Della said he exclaimed "Oh I know what you mean. You mean the Almighty, but the Almighty has nothing to do with this war!" Such blasphemy silenced me completely and I felt it was wrong or at least imprudent to talk to such a creature.

We hear of unrestrained plunder and destruction in every direction. The poor nigs suffer severely and I fear we are all destined to feel the pangs of hunger and poverty, but after hearing that man talk I had rather do anything, suffer anything than submit. But oh to think of the noble, glorious men we love by [sic] the hands of those wretches. Tho' everything looks black around yet I feel that we must succeed. I pray it is not presumption.

Bessie in Love and War

Great relief was felt by the Allstons and their neighbors when the enemy troops finally left the area. Soon afterward, Brutus arrived from Loch Adele, their plantation in North Carolina, to report that part of Sherman's army had camped there for a week, plundering and destroying, and that they had "left the negroes without a thing to eat." Bessie's diary entry for March 12 gave details of their doings at the plantation.

Diary

Sunday March 12th 1865. The day is bright and beautiful. Everything looks full of peace and joy, and thank Heaven there are none of the Enemy now near us. This morning we all walked to church and got there in full time. There was not a vehicle of any sort except a mule cart at the church. Everyone looked cheerful. Indeed, I the reaction has made everyone feel brighter than usual. The sense of relief is so great that I feel as tho an immense burden had been lifted from my shoulders. Everyone of course has suffered more or less. We I think got off lightly here, but we hear terrible accounts of their doings in No[rth] Ca[rolina]. Not a bushel of corn left on the place! Not a mule or cow or turkey or chicken! The gin house burnt with 18 tierces of salt and a good deal of cotton. On leaving they set fire to the house but the negroes put it out. They have destroyed everything in the house, furniture, pictures, glasses, the marble cellarette. They took the marble off and broke it to atoms. Some beautiful old English oak chairs they smashed and took the seats off with them! Indeed there is nothing left on the place but a little rough rice. Only three boys went with the Enemy. Mamma feels it terribly and says ruin is inevitable and so it is, for without work animals there is no possibility of making even <u>half</u> provision for the people.

We hear dreadful rumors of doings below but have nothing that is reliable. Yesterday Mamma and I

1865

walked into the village to see Mr. Coker. He was not there at first but we saw Mr. Pringle and Rebecca. Like us they fared pretty well at the dwelling house, but every bit of Mr. P's wine (a great quantity) is gone. The Yankees and all his negroes became perfectly drunk on it. Fortunately the river divided them from the plantation, so they did not feel the bad effects. All their glass and china at Mr. Coker's was smashed. I saw the fragments and it was almost enough to make one cry. Rebecca was very cheerful however. Every horse they had is gone, the hiding place betrayed by one of the negroes. The only two horses we had after sending the rest to [Butler] were saved along with Mr. Evans' horses and returned to us today—Marie and Kitty. They are brown mares and not very strong.

Brutus came down from N.C. two days ago. He had seen dear Charly at Wadesboro and marched six miles with him to carry his kit. He says he was well, but had to throw away his clothes because of the hard marching and so was very ragged and dirty.

Later in March, a few days after the return of Brutus, Mrs. Allston decided that she must go to Loch Adele in North Carolina. Her friend Mr. Evans advised her against it, but, unable to persuade her, he offered to accompany her and her party on horseback. Bessie's memoir described the horrid desolation left behind by Sherman's army:

> So at daylight the next morning we started; mamma and I in the carriage with a basket of cooked food, Daddy Aleck driving and Brutus behind him on the box, Mr. Evans riding beside the carriage. It was an awful experience, as it must always be to travel in the track of a destroying army. To begin with, the road was a quagmire. It took an experienced driver like Daddy Aleck to get us through, and even with all his care Brutus and Mr. Evans had often to get a rail from the

fences along the road and pry our wheels out of the bog. We were never out of the sight of dead things, and the stench was almost unbearable. Dead horses all along the way and, here and there, a leg or an arm sticking out of hastily made too-shallow grave. Along the way ten cows dead in one pen, and then eight or ten calves dead in another. Dead hogs everywhere; the effort being to starve the inhabitants out, no living thing was left in a very abundant country. It is a country of small farms, just two-roomed houses; all now tightly shut up, no sign of life. Wells with all means of drawing water destroyed.

At Loch Adele, where some of Sherman's troops had camped, Mrs. Allston discovered some food supplies which had been hidden away, and was relieved to know that no one would starve. As Bessie recorded in *Chronicles,* she "made arrangements for provisions for them to be brought to the farm every week." When the Allstons returned to Croly Hill the next day, they found Charles there. He was very ill, but soon recovered for the most part.

A letter that Mrs. Allston received from Elizabeth Blyth Weston described alarming conditions in Georgetown District.[198] Dated March 17, 1865, the letter reported, among many other things, that the plantation of Henry A. Middleton had been burned to the ground by U.S. troops, that some planters had been arrested, and that the plantation of the Pyatts, who had fled to Georgetown, "was given up to the Negroes at once."[199]

Many of the defenseless Georgetown District plantations were plundered and dismantled at the close of the war, and some,

---

[198] The city of Georgetown had been captured by a U.S. navy squadron on February 24, and a garrison of between 600 and 800 troops was established there

[199] Easterby, *The South Carolina Rice Plantation,* 206. Henry Augustus Middleton (1793-1887) owned Weehaw Plantation on the Black River. His daughter reported in a letter of March 1865, "Papa was turned out of his house. Capt. Pierce of the 157th New York Volunteers thus addressed him, 'You damn old rebel you, get out of your house this minute. I mean to burn it down and set you afloat in the world.' Then he took his bonds, money and everything else he found and burnt the house." Stokes, *South Carolina Civilians in Sherman's Path,* 58. The Pyatts owned Rosemont, and an adjacent plantation called Kensington, both of which were pillaged and vandalized.

including Keithfield, were burned to the ground. In a memoir left by Alicia Shubrick Trapier, she wrote of events at Windsor Plantation, her family home on the Black River, recalling that the U.S. troops who arrived there "soon began their work of loot and destruction." After the house was thoroughly pillaged, the commanding officer ordered it to be burned, but two of the Trapier ladies managed to change his mind. Another family member, the Rev. Richard Shubrick Trapier, was arrested by the soldiers, tied up, and marched to Georgetown, where he was jailed for about three weeks. He had been accused of putting poison in some of the wine at Windsor Plantation, but was eventually acquitted of these false charges.[200]

The letter of March 17 quoted above also reported that "The Revnd Mr Trappier [*sic*] was long in prison and threatened with hanging for poisoning the wine…he is again at Liberty but his family have been stripped of everything and the faithful Servants who wished to remain with them were carried off by force."

In April, Bessie was deeply grieved to learn of the death of her beloved cousin Hal (Henry R. Lesesne).

Diary

April 11th. Last night Arnoldus came in suddenly with May Parker. They were direct from Raleigh and oh what sad sad news they bring. Poor fellow, I know that death would have been in his eyes easier, but then to fall in an unsuccessful struggle is so sad, on the 16th March. I wish I could remember what I was doing and thinking of that day—Hal. Hal, I am so sorry I will miss you very much my friend, th[ough] if I had known what was before you that evening when I said goodbye I should have not been so careful to hide how much it hurt me to see you go.[201] I was afraid then you would

---

200   Alicia Shubrick Trapier's memoir is found in the Trapier Family Papers at the South Caroliniana Library.

201   Hal was Bessie's cousin Henry Russell Lesesne, who was killed at the fighting at Averasboro, North Carolina, on March 16, 1865. The son of Harriette Petigru and Henry

not understand it. Killed instantly, a ball through the head, and oh horror left on the field. The Enemy took possession and our troops retreated. That all we know, probably all will ever know. Little I thought that evening when you said "Remember if I have some little wound I shall call you to nurse me" and I laughingly said "yes." That no kind hand or gentle word would soothe you anymore. Poor Aunt Harrie. Her first born, long wished for child. I can only cry when I think of him. God have mercy on his soul. It makes me [mad] to think that what influence I had I did not I fear use sufficiently to try and turn his thoughts heavenward. God forgive me. Oh if he had only been wounded. It would be so different! But then <u>His ways</u> are best we are told and one must strive to clutch the great anchor and cling to it. I can't cry. Oh, it seems hard, unfeeling, and yet I loved my cousin dearly, and I doubt if anyone but his Father and Mother will miss him as I will. I don't realize it yet.

Charley is better, downstairs today. This day week [sic] he went to [bed] and we feared Typhoid fever, but he is almost [hardy] again. Yes I remember Thursday 16th we were in No[rth] Ca[rolina]. Friday we came down and met Charly here. He had come the day before on a leave of ten days. As soon as he is able he will return to Spartanburg.[202]

Shortly after Bessie's April 11th diary entry, the war ended. The news of General Robert E. Lee's surrender at Appomattox, she wrote in *Chronicles*, was "crushing and numbing to all my being."

Deas Lesesne, he was captain of a company in the 1st South Carolina Artillery Regiment.

202 Young militia soldiers and cadets were ordered to a camp of instruction (training) at Spartanburg, South Carolina, under the command of Captain Charles E. Chichester. The cadets were later ordered to Greenville, South Carolina.

Chapter Six:

AFTER THE WAR

IN HIS WILL, ROBERT F.W. ALLSTON left his plantations to his five children. Chicora Wood was left to Charles; Guendalos, to Benjamin; Ditchfield, to Jane; Exchange, to Bessie; and Waterford, to Adele. Another plantation, Nightingale Hall, was to be sold for the benefit of the heirs. Mrs. Allston received the house on Meeting Street in Charleston along with a bequest of money. Despite all these properties, however, Mr. Allston's estate was heavily in debt, and, as the executrix, his widow struggled to deal with it by eventually renting out some of the properties, and putting others under the direction of her son Benjamin.[203]

Just after the war's end, the Allstons faced other difficulties and challenges—among them, as Bessie noted in her diary entries of May 1865—dealing with the newly freed slaves, and taking the oath of allegiance to the United States.[204] In that month, she and her mother and brother Charles set out from Croly Hill for Georgetown District, John Julius Pringle joining them, too. After visits to Plantersville and Georgetown, the Allstons were invited to stay at the Pringle plantation, White House. Mrs. Allston then visited her family plantations. Because she had not been present at Chicora Wood when United States naval vessels landed troops along the Pee Dee River to take control of the plantation lands in February 1865, the freedmen had been allowed to take what they

---

203 Easterby, *The South Carolina Rice Plantation*, 18.
204 Submitting to this hated oath was necessary for certain legal protections and property ownership and transactions.

wanted from the place as abandoned property. In a letter to the U.S. authorities in Georgetown, Mrs. Allston wrote that "my house at Chicora Wood plantation has been robbed of every article of furniture and much defaced and injured also all my provisions of meat, lard, coffee and tea taken."[205]

Diary

Left Croly Hill Thursday, May 11th. Spent the first night at Gen. Harlee's, the next morning started somewhat late, but reached Mr. Sampson's this side of the ferry in good time.[206] They were very kind and much to my annoyance refused any compensation. As we were ready to leave the next morning Dot was taken very sick.[207] I thought the little thing was gone, but she seemed relieved sufficiently to continue the journey, Mr. P[ringle] leading her and Charley in the carriage. Mr. [Z] undertook to show us a new road, saying the bridges were down on the regular road. He put us in blind sort of path and then left us. Had it not been for skillful guidance we should surely have lost our way. The road was so rough and Dot so languid we did not get farther than Mr. Grier's. We were relieved to hear in Carver's Bay that things were quieter down here than we had expected. In the morning (today) we came on to the village and found the W[eston]'s just finished breakfast. We walked up to the house and found it entirely empty and in a very [rowdy] condition all together. In the afternoon Mrs. P, M, and Mr. P. came in and Mamma agreed with Mrs. P. to go to Geo[rgetown] the next morning.[208]

---

205 Easterby, *The South Carolina Rice Plantation*, 209.

206 William Wallace Harllee (1812-1897) owned a plantation called Sunnyside near the Pee Dee River, and this may have been where the Allstons stopped for a night. Harllee was a general in the South Carolina Militia.

207 Dot was a mare owned by the Allstons.

208 "Mrs. P." was Jane Lynch Pringle, a widow, and the mother of John Julius Pringle ("Mr. P.") and Mary Izard Pringle ("M."). Mary later married a French count, Yvan Marie Edmond

After the War

Monday 15th. We drove down to W[hite] H[ouse] to meet Mrs. P[ringle]. We waited some minutes before M. and herself appeared in the mule buggy. Mrs. P. went with Mamma to town and I drove home with Mary. Late in the afternoon they returned from town, Mamma having done the deed and become a citizen of the U.S. I was [illegible words] tho' I expected it felt as tho' a barrier had been raised between us, so I still feel [illegible words] everyone who has taken the oath tho' it is the only thing to be done. Tuesday Mamma and I went to N[ightingale] H[all] where she took the keys from Mack without any opposition then we went on to Chicora and oh the desolation but I won't speak of that. This is only a record of facts, leaving sentiments out of the question entirely if I can. The house is standing, not many shutters or doors left, no piece of furniture in it, the front steps gone. The whole place looks like a ruin tho' beautiful as ever. Mamma sent for Primus (whom they made head man), looked through the barns and then told him to give her the keys. He laughed heartily and refused. She reiterated her demand in a very solemn manner and finding that he still refused she became much excited and threatened him with the consequences of a persistent refusal. He at last seemed intimidated and gave them up. We returned to W[hite] H[ouse] for dinner.

Wednesday we returned to Chicora and found things looking less hostile. Primus' manner was quite subdued and Richard and Jacob, Paul and Peter quite respectful. Mamma had them to take out the needful service and place it in an empty barn of which she gave Primus the key. Returned to W[hite] H[ouse] again to late dinner. Thursday we did not go out but spent a pleasant day indoors. Cut out my calico. The next

---

Colas Des Francs de Polignac (1850-1912). Their wedding was held in Georgetown, S.C., on April 29, 1873.

morning Mamma said we must leave so we pack [*sic*] our bag and took our leave, stopping on the way up at Guendalos to take the keys there. We drove to the barnyard and saw a good many young people but could not find either the head man Jacob or his wife. Sam B. was quite as usual. We came up to Plantersville and found we would be obliged to spend the night at Cousin Lizzie's as the house was not yet dry and perfectly empty. All this time dear C[aroline] was the greatest possible comfort, working with energy and judgment. Saturday we moved home and gradually the furniture was gotten from Lavinia, but only half of it about.[209]

In her memoir *Chronicles,* Bessie gave details of her family's visit shortly after the end of the war to White House Plantation, an estate located "twelve miles south of Plantersville, on the Pee Dee River." This plantation, formerly the home of South Carolina statesman Joel Roberts Poinsett and his wife Mary Izard Pringle, had been raided several times, but had not suffered as severely as Chicora Wood. After Mrs. Poinsett's death in 1857, John Julius Izard Pringle (her son by her first marriage) inherited White House. When he died in 1864, it became the property of his widow Jane Lynch Pringle, the mother of John Julius Pringle. Bessie wrote:

I had never been to the White House before, though I had always heard of it as very beautiful; a picturesque, rambling house with three gables, set facing the river about 200 yards away, in a most beautiful garden, which had been planted by Mr. Poinsett, who was a specialist on gardens, a botanist. The White House was even more beautiful than I had imagined. As soon as you left the road you entered a lane bordered on each side with the most luxuriant climbing roses, now in riotous bloom, long garlands of white roses swaying in the breeze, high up, and quarrelling for supremacy with long garlands

---

209 In *Chronicles,* Bessie described Caroline as a housemaid at Chicora Wood. "Maum Lavinia" was described as a "competent house-servant" with a "terrible temper."

AFTER THE WAR

of pink roses. This lane took you direct to the Pee Dee River, where you made a sharp turn on the edge of the river, which had here a sand beach like the seashore. The effect was delightful; on the left the river, only a few feet away, on the right a green lawn, until you came to the vegetable-garden. A picture garden! All the vegetables sedately in straight rows, and having nothing to do with each other. The French artichokes standing in stately stiff rows, not so much as glancing at the waving asparagus bed, nor the rows of pale-green mammoth roses, which turn out to be heads of lettuce. I had never seen a vegetable-garden which was ornamental before. While I was taking it in we entered the flower-garden, with a wilderness of roses, azaleas, camellias, and other beautiful shrubs and plants...

In *Chronicles,* Bessie also recalled that, one day during their visit, Mrs. Pringle and Mrs. Allston took a carriage to Georgetown in order to take the oath of allegiance there (as she had noted in her diary), leaving her with Mary Pringle and her brothers at White House. It was an especially memorable day for Bessie, and for her future husband, whose presence, she wrote, "cast a spell over me."

I was embroidering a waist in black silk, to make a Russian blouse out of the everlasting purple calico we were all wearing. As I sewed in a big chair in the beautiful library, filled with most delightful books, exquisite engravings on the walls and marble busts around the room, Mr. Pringle read aloud to me. He picked up the first book his hand came upon,—I think it was "Eugene Aram." But the book was nothing; it was his voice, so beautifully modulated, and his presence, safe back from the awful danger, and in his own beautiful home. It cast a spell over me; and long afterwards he told me he had no idea of what he was reading; nothing of it entered his mind; it was the simple fact of having me sitting there in his own home, sewing as if I belonged there, that intoxicated him, so that he was afraid to speak, and so took refuge in reading! So there we were, a pair of idiots, in a fool's paradise, some might think, but such moments are immortal. Soul speaks to soul, though no voice be heard.

After Benjamin Allston returned to South Carolina with his Texas bride Ellen, he took over the management of Chicora Wood in order to make it productive again, but there, and at the other family plantations, there were persistent problems with the newly emancipated workers, who were restless and dissatisfied with the terms of their labor contracts with the landowners.[210] Benjamin's first child, a daughter named Adele, died in 1865, and his wife was in poor health for a long while after giving birth. Bessie, who was fond of Ellen, nursed her in her illness.

In *Chronicles,* Bessie included some excerpts from one of her diaries, writing in Plantersville on August 1, 1865: "My days are so happy. I cut and contrive new garments out of old, and sew and dream as I sew." Less than two weeks later, however, another diary entry tells a very different story. One of her other surviving diaries, which consists of a number of loose pages damaged by scorch marks, has entries for 1865, 1866, and 1867, and one of them, written in early August 1865, bears witness to Bessie's deep unhappiness with her shattered world, and with herself.

Diary

Mrs. Pringle and Lynch have been here this morning, pleasanter than usual. Poor John Tucker's funeral takes place this afternoon at four.[211] What a terrible death! Killed on a hunt! Poor Mrs. Tucker, Mamma says she

---

210 "Ben, with the assistance of his brother Charles, endeavored to operate at least four of the Allston plantations—Chicora Wood, Guendalos, Nightingale Hall, and Pipe Down—in a desperate effort to save the estate, which by 1866 was $200,000 in debt ... Despite the best efforts of Ben and Charles, the rice crops on the Allston plantations proved to be disappointing in 1866." Scarborough, *The Allstons of Chicora Wood,* 162.

211 John Hyrne Tucker (1827-1865), a Georgetown District planter and physician, died on August 8, 1865. His wife, Sarah Tams Tucker (1830-1903), was the daughter of Sampson Tams and Ann H. Tams of Pennsylvania.

was wonderfully in love with him when they were married. She is at the north and in all probability will not hear for weeks. It is very sad. This period is filled with horrors, not only here but everywhere. I often wonder now if there <u>is</u> such a thing as <u>happiness</u> in the world. For my part I think there is not. I see no one around me happy, except those who are kept up by the mere force of animal life and spirits, and those who haven't that blessing strive to appear content and happy, and [first] acquaintances they succeed, but as soon as one knows them better the skeleton peeps out. It is such a blessing that people make the effort to conceal, for if everyone knew the real state of everyone else's mind this world w[oul]d be the saddest state possible. Now I used to be blessed with spirits enough for three reasonable beings, but malheureusement pour moi[212] I have exhausted my fund w[hic]h I and everyone else thought inexhaustible and now at twenty find myself inexpressibly depressed and weary—of what? Of myself principally and then everybody else. There is a lack of <u>something</u> in my composition, energy, will, force of character, I don't know w[hic]h perhaps all. Anyway something w[hic]h will make me a useless cipher in life. This I have sense enough to see without strength to alter it. It is this hopeless despondency about myself that depresses me.

Facing many financial difficulties, Mrs. Allston began making plans in the summer of 1865 to open a school for girls at her house in Charleston, hoping that this venture would bring in at least a moderate income. At this time, Mrs. Allston and most of her children were living at their house in Plantersville, where, after a short while, Bessie seemed to shake off her despondency. She began to enjoy riding parties and other social outings, embracing natural, youthful desires for life and its joys after four traumatic years of war and bereavement. In August, Mrs. Allston made a trip to

---

212 Unfortunately for me.

Bessie in Love and War

Charleston to secure a contractor to make repairs to her Meeting Street house, which had been struck by several shells during the long enemy bombardment of the city.

After her father's death, Bessie had resolved to devote herself to her mother's comfort and support, but when she learned that Mrs. Allston expected her to teach at the school in Charleston, she found herself very upset. In *Chronicles,* quoting from a diary of 1865, she wrote:

> Aug. 25th. A letter from Mamma today has upset me completely. She has been successful in getting the house repaired. A contractor who knew her well and had worked for Papa and done up the house the last time, undertook to do all the work without any payment now; but when he has finished, Mamma will give him her note promising to pay as soon as she can. This has lifted a great load, but the tremendous announcement is that she has determined to open a boarding and day school, and she expects me to *teach*! The minute I read the letter I wrote, 'Mamma, I cannot teach. Don't ask me to do it. I just hate the thought. Besides, I don't know enough of any one thing to teach. I cannot, indeed, I cannot.' Now that I have sent the letter I am awfully ashamed, and when we were riding this afternoon, we fell a little behind the others and I told Mr. P[ringle]. He seemed so shocked and surprised. Altogether I am miserable. Am I really just a butterfly? Is my love of pleasure the strongest thing about me? What an awful thought. I try to pray, but I don't want to pray. I just want to be for a while like a flower in the sun. I want to open and feel the glow and the beauty and the joy of existing, even if I know I have to wither and die sometime.

Bessie felt ashamed when her mother wrote back to her with gentle words, offering no reproaches for her "petulance and miserable selfishness." She continued her diary entries in *Chronicles* in September, relating a curious exchange with John Julius Pringle:

> Sept. 3rd. We cannot have any service in the dear little old log church, for Mr. Trapier will not pray for the President of the United States, and so we have not the pleasure and comfort of church.[213]
>
> Mr. P[ringle] comes every day and reads aloud to me. It is really unique. I sit inside the window and sew on my ingenious remakings of old things and he sits outside of the window and reads, "He knew He was Right."[214] It is perfectly delightful for me, it is so much easier than talking. People are so disagreeable, the village is all saying we are engaged. I know he is hearing it all the time, as I am, and it is so awkward for both. I thought it would be easier if I referred lightly to it, so this morning, sewing very fast, pricking my first finger brutally, I said, "Last evening I was walking in the village and heard something so absurdly ridiculous." I got no farther, for in a solemn, hurt voice, from across the window sill, there came, "I'm sorry it seemed so ridiculous to you. It did not seem so to me." Then I took refuge in immoderate laughter, after which I said, "Please go on with the book." But I felt I had been defeated in my effort to make things more comfortable.

Despite her attraction to Pringle, Bessie did little to encourage his attentions besides allowing him to spend time with her. She

---

213 This was the Rev. Richard Shubrick Trapier (1811-1895), who resided at Windsor Plantation. The church referred to was a wooden summer chapel for Prince Frederick Parish in Plantersville. The occupying military authorities in Charleston and elsewhere had informed clergymen that ministers who omitted prayers for the U.S. president would not be allowed to officiate in their churches.

214 *He Knew He Was Right* was a novel by Anthony Trollope. It was serialized in 1867-1868, and published as a book in 1869. It appears that Bessie added this misplaced detail about their reading when she was writing *Chronicles of Chicora Wood* many years later, since the date of her diary entry is 1865. Dr. Anne M. Blythe noted that Bessie sometimes revised diary entries in *A Woman Rice Planter*. Bessie did the same in *Chronicles*.

seemed to know his feelings for her, but appeared to be ambivalent and perhaps even fearful about her strong attraction to him. Referring to him as "my friend," she wrote about him again in her diary in October, as she prepared to leave Plantersville and join her mother in Charleston.

> Oct. 20th. The last few days have been trying. I have had so much trouble to keep on the surface. I am going tomorrow. Brother [Ben] will drive me to Georgetown to take the boat. My irresponsible life ends. It has not lasted long, for, Brother being away, I had all the copying of Papa's will to send to the different members of the family, and the lists of the negroes and the plantations and all the property to make, and it is only these two months, since Brother has been at home and has taken charge of everything, that I have been able to enjoy being young and foolish. I love dancing and I love admiration and I love to be gay; but all the time, underneath all that, I am so terribly serious, so terribly in earnest that I find the other girls do not understand me and the men are startled and puzzled—all but my friend, and I have to be so fiercely foolish and on the surface with him if I am to prevent a catastrophe, and I must prevent it.

The "catastrophe" could only have been a declaration of love and a proposal of marriage by John Julius Pringle.

For Bessie's first weeks in Charleston, she stayed at the home of her elderly Aunt Jane Petigru, the widow of James Louis Petigru. The Charleston to which she had returned was much changed from the place she had known before, having been occupied by Union troops since mid-February 1865, when the Confederate defenders evacuated, uncertain as to whether Sherman's army would descend upon the city. The besieging enemy forces quickly took possession of Charleston; and the property of its residents, most of whom had also evacuated, was left open to the depredations of the soldiers and other opportunists. Many homes were pillaged.

After the War

For a long period after the war, Charleston was under military rule, but gradually, Charlestonians began to return to the city. Their circumstances were greatly altered, almost universally for the worse, as many suffered under severe economic hardships. Social events eventually resumed, albeit on a much reduced scale—yet Bessie's experiences testify that the young people, especially those of courting age, could enjoy themselves despite the lack of luxuries.

By the first of December, Bessie was residing in the beautiful family house on Meeting Street, which her mother would operate as "Mrs. R. F. W. Allston's Boarding and Day School for Young Ladies."[215] Its doors opened in January 1866, and before long, much to her surprise, Bessie discovered she had a knack for teaching, and that she actually enjoyed it. Her sister Jane and brother Charles were also with their mother in Charleston.

Finding old and new friends in the city, Bessie eventually also began to experience "the great and unexpected pleasure of going into society," which started when she began to act regularly as chaperone for some of the young ladies who were pupils at her mother's school. She wrote of this in *Chronicles*:

> I wish I had time to tell of my many friends; they were all such nice men, who had fought through the war, and now were not ashamed to take any kind of honest work to enable them to help their mothers and sisters. There were literally butchers and bakers, and candlestick-makers, but all thorough, true gentlemen, and most of them beautiful dancers. The only public balls we had that year [1867] were the three balls given by the Cotillion Club. They were in the South Carolina Hall, with a fine waxed floor and good band of music, but very mild refreshments.

---

215 The "Terms for Boarding Pupils" per session found in the initial school prospectus gave a cost of over $250 for board, tuition in English and French, pew rent, stationery, the use of a piano, and laundry services. There were additional charges for instruction in music, drawing, dancing, German, and other accomplishments.

> The private parties were too delightful; the young men of the family giving the party always waxed the floor, and they became experts in doing it, and that was really the sole thing absolutely necessary to the success of a party. We were sure of good music, for there were four or five girls going into society that played delightfully for dancing. The refreshments generally consisted of rolls, handed in dishes of exquisite china, and water in very dainty glasses. At one or two houses we had the rare treat of coffee, but that did not often happen, and when the rolls appeared just before the German, they were welcome, and greatly enjoyed, for we were all working hard, and living none too high. In the winter the only recreation, except the dancing, was walking on the Battery in the afternoon. We made engagements for this, just as we did for a German, generally with girl friends, for the men at work did not get off for the afternoons.[216]

On Sundays, it was common for couples to walk and sit near the water at Chisolm's Mill, and Bessie observed that many "lads and lasses" became engaged at that spot.[217] She received her first proposal of marriage there.

> I can never forget the shock of my first proposal, which took place down there. I had worked so hard before I left the country to prevent the asking of that question, and had succeeded so well, knowing all the time in my secret heart that I had done so because I doubted my power to say no with sufficient firmness if the fateful words were spoken, and had put all such thoughts out of my mind entirely; I went out as a chaperon, enjoying myself as a married woman would do; I

---

216 The "German," or cotillion, was a type of social dance based on an English country dance, or contredanse.

217 This mill was located at the western end of Tradd Street near the Ashley River (now the location of a Coast Guard station).

knew there was only one man in the world that I would ever marry, and not quite sure that I could even marry him, but I forgot that other people did not know that. I had a great deal of attention and a great many friends, but never thought of them as possible lovers; so when one evening, sitting on a pile of squared logs which were far from comfortable, watching the tide come in, with the most glorious sunset clouds reflected in the water, and we had stopped talking for some time, and my thoughts were far away, Mr. Blank asked me to marry him, I just gasped with horror and exclaimed: "Oh, how awful! How could you spoil all our delightful friendship in this way! I am so distressed!" But he said: "Miss Bessie, this is very extraordinary conduct on your part! What did you think that I was coming to see you all the time for, and playing chess regularly once a week for, and following you about all the time at the parties, and doing everything in the world I could for you? I have never cared for any one else, and I never thought you could fail to understand my devotion."

"Oh," I repeated, "it is too awful! You know, your dear sister was my best friend, and I liked you because of that, and I thought that was what made you like me, and I liked to be with you because you looked like her and reminded me of her; I have missed her so ever since she died. But now I see how blind and selfish I have been." We had an awful walk home and parted at the steps, and he never came to see me again.[218]

After this unfortunate incident, Bessie resolved to become more careful of her friendships with men, and yet, despite her good intentions, there was another young man in her life whose

---

[218] No conclusive information could be found on "Mr. Blank." It is likely that it was his real name, although there are alternate spellings of the surname (Blanc, Blanck, Blanq, etc.) in records. There were individuals in Charleston who had that surname, a few of whom were Jewish, and the city directory of 1869 lists a "Henry Blank," a clerk. The 1870 South Carolina census lists a John Blank, age 27, in Charleston. Oddly enough, in *Chronicles of Chicora Wood*, a "Mr. Blank" is also mentioned as a suitor of Bessie's mother, and later, her sister Adele.

friendship also grew into ardent but unwanted devotion that led to a marriage proposal. Details about this relationship are found in the loose, scorched pages of one of Bessie's diaries, on several undated sheets and others dated 1867. The young man was George Herbert Sass. A native of Charleston, he graduated from the College of Charleston in 1868 with a degree in law, but he was also a poet who would later publish his works under the pen name Barton Gray. Bessie wrote of him in her diary:

> This month is gliding by very rapidly [and] it is pleasant to think that in six weeks more we will enjoy the quiet of home. [I] have made lately a progress in acquaintance which I think will give me great pleasure. Mr. Sass's poetry is certainly very beautiful that is parts of it. I think him by far the cleverest man (except Uncle and Cousin Johnston)[219] I have ever known. He is conceited but this I think will in the course of time wear off altogether, and is already diminishing. He either pretends to have or really has (sometimes I think one and sometimes the other) a very high opinion of my mental powers, and speaks to me on subjects that no one else ever does. The other evening he brought me his last poem "A Dream of Old" to read. I read it with great pleasure and found it very beautiful. It is a meditative piece simply on the possible grandeur of man at first, and then gradually fixing on the character of Moses and traces faintly the outline of his life and death [and] mysterious burial. Finally it winds up with a word of encouragement to all who earnestly strive for the noble and true. The whole thing is wonderfully pure and truthful to my mind. There is a solemn earnestness in its tone that speaks directly to the soul.

Letters found in the Allston family correspondence document indicate that Sass was also a good friend of Bessie's sister

---

219   Bessie's uncle James Louis Petigru, and her cousin James Johnston Pettigrew.

After the War

Jane. An undated note from him to "Miss Jane" invited her and "Miss Bessie" to play a game of croquet at his house one afternoon. He likely courted Jane at some point, too, but it is certain that he entertained feelings of a deeper nature for Bessie. Two loose sheets of Bessie's diary recount his proposal of marriage. These two pages, which seem to be consecutive (and more damaged by scorching than the others), begin with an entry dated March 13th, 1867:

> I feel very sad today, and in vain I try to get rid of my depression. Yesterday was my evening for walking with Mr. S[ass] and I made up my mind to tell him that it must be our last walk for some time to come, as the reports about us had become so numerous and were so generally believed. I thought that the only way to put a stop to them. We took a quiet walk up to see the bride Mrs. Lock (Hennie Holmes) and then came home.[220] He asked me to go up [stairs] not into the room where "everybody" was. I refused at first, but at last said, "Well for the last time" and ordered the light carried up and went to change my dress. He wanted to talk first but I insisted on reading the Italian first, Metastasio's "Demoofoonte." We read tho he [illegible words] then he stopped and asked me the [illegible words] what I had said at the door. [Illegible words] him simply and truly my reasons, how [I] could not bear to be talked about in connection with anyone and that I hoped the total cessation of intercourse might put a stop to all talk and then later we might resume our pleasant walks occasionally. He asked me then if I could not see another way of putting a stop to them. I said no, none. He said, "Miss Bessie, you know, you must know that I love you better than anything in the world. I would have spoken long long ago but that I could only ask a very long engagement and my position is such that I scarcely felt I

---

[220] This was Henrietta Holmes (1848-1919), who married Arthur Hall Locke (1846-1905).

had the right, but there are some times that we cannot think of what we ought to do and now I beg and entreat you to verify the reports and thus put an end to them, can't you Miss Bessie?" I could have cried heartily but I only shook my head. He went on, "I have felt it growing in me day by day stronger and stronger. When you went to Georgetown I felt it first in full force. I was utterly wretched until you came back. Oh Miss Bessie, examine your heart well. I can't believe you can be indifferent. Have you thought how we are [illegible] constantly and be only strangers to each other, we who have been such friends. There is not a thought or feeling with which you have not been connected."

Bessie did not record George Herbert Sass's proposal in *Chronicles of Chicora Wood*. She mentioned him only briefly in her memoir, recalling that she read Italian literature with her friend "Mr. Sass" in Charleston.[221]

Bessie's sister-in-law Ellen Allston, who was living at Guendalos Plantation, wrote to Mrs. Allston in Charleston relating news about family and friends, mentioning she had recently heard that "Bessie had refused Mr. Sass." Ellen added disapprovingly, "Tell Bessie I believe she is a flirt no matter what she says to the contrary."

In another letter from Ellen, written from Plantersville, she told Mrs. Allston she hoped that Bessie, in whose company she always took "great pleasure," would come to the village for the summer.[222] She also confided her views about Bessie and John Julius Pringle, writing:

> I still think Julius Pringle is seriously attached to Bessie but he does not wish to risk a refusal and she gives him little reason to hope for future things. I think this is best "entre nous" dear Mother for I know

---

221   In *Chronicles*, Bessie also wrote of her love for poetry. She always kept with her a copy of Chaucer's *Canterbury Tales* and Homer's *Iliad*.

222   Both letters from Ellen Allston are undated but were likely written in June 1867.

After the War

Bessie is certainly not the least contrary of her sex and any family discussions do more harm than good. If she thought all the rest desired something it is more than likely she would be opposed to it and I for one would be very glad for her to marry Julius P. I know him very well and think most highly of him both as regards intellect and principles. He has an outlying side of worldliness 'tis true but is the real metal for all that. He has plainly given me to understand how he feels and I tell you but do not want to tell Bessie. She would probably abuse her power more than she does already and I am really inclined to think she has more coquetry in her nature than is strictly orthodox.

In 1868, Bessie's younger sister Jane "made her debut" in Charleston society, and was much admired, especially by one "special friend" named Bayard Clinch.[223] Bessie continued to chaperone some of the school girls at parties and balls, and, once in a while, John Julius Pringle would make an appearance in the city. She recalled in *Chronicles*:

> My own special friend was working so hard on the rice-planation in the country that he did not very often get to town, and then, though I always knew when I entered a ballroom if he was there, by a queer little feeling, I always treated him with great coolness and never gave him more than one dance in an evening, for there were two kinds of people I could not bear to dance with—the people whom I disliked and those I liked too much, and he was the only one in the second class.

Bessie spent the summer of 1868 with friends in Virginia, and then returned to Charleston to continue her duties at her mother's school. The following year would see the last term of Mrs. Allston's establishment, which had not turned out to be quite the success she

---
223 This may have been Nicholas Bayard Clinch (1832-1888), a former Confederate officer.

had hoped for. She decided that she would exercise a legal right she had as the widow of Robert F.W. Allston to give up the Charleston house and claim as her dower Chicora Wood Plantation instead. The whole family was happy about this decision, Bessie recalled, "for the idea of giving up Chicora was dreadful."

In late February or early March 1869, Mrs. Allston received a letter from a cousin in Brooklyn, New York. His name was John Earl Allston, and he wished to offer help to her and her family by way of repaying an old kindness. Part of the letter is reproduced in *Chronicles:*

> MY DEAR COUSIN:
>
> I have placed to your credit in the Bank of Charleston the sum of $5,000, which I hope will be useful to you.
>
> You need feel no sense of obligation in receiving it, for it is not one-half of what my Cousin Robert, your husband, did for me and mine in the past. When my mother's house was to be sold over her head, he bought it and gave it to her, and many other things he did for us, and it is a great pleasure to me to be able to do this for his widow and family.

This unexpected windfall was a great blessing, and it came at just the right time, as Mrs. Allston would have to spend money to make repairs to the house at Chicora Wood, which had been "all torn to pieces," and buy necessary implements, supplies, and livestock that were needed for the plantation.

In *Chronicles,* Bessie related how her family prepared to leave Charleston for Chicora Wood, revealing she had made some plans of her own that did not include her family plantation home:

> The packing up of all our belongings was a tremendous business, but in this as in everything else Charley was most efficient, and he did it with a good heart, as it was the greatest happiness to him that we were moving back to Chicora, and that he was going

to plant the place. Jinty was also perfectly happy, the thought of being able to live on horseback once more filled her with joy. I, only, was downhearted; to me human nature had become more interesting than plain nature, and people more fascinating than plants. So I determined to apply for a place as a music-teacher in the town of Union, S.C., which had been held by a very charming friend of mine who played beautifully, Caro Ravenel.[224] The family did not approve of my doing this as mamma thought I needed rest; anyway, were to go to the pineland for the summer and I would not have to leave for Union until the autumn.

I remember well the last Sunday we were to be in Charleston; during the service I was so moved I had to put down my heavy veil to conceal my tears!

Bessie and her family left Charleston in the summer of 1869 and resided for a while at their summer cottage in Plantersville before returning to Chicora Wood. On August 22, 1869, Mrs. Allston wrote to her daughter Adele in Charleston, reporting that "Bessie is well in health, but not amiable. She is irritable."

Bessie's plans to teach music in Union were never carried out. On the same day Mrs. Allston penned her letter of August 22, John Julius Pringle asked Bessie to marry him, and she accepted.

---

[224] This was Caroline Ravenel (1844-1889), who married Daniel Elliott Huger Smith (1846-1932).

White House Plantation on the Pee Dee River, circa 1900. The house burned in 1919. From the collections of the S.C. Historical Society.

Chapter Seven:

Married Life

BESSIE WAS NOW TO MARRY into a cosmopolitan, once wealthy family dominated by Mrs. Jane Lynch Pringle. She was the widow of John Julius Izard Pringle, who had spent much of his life in Europe. He owned Greenfield Plantation on the Black River in Georgetown District, and, after his mother's death in 1857, he also took possession of White House Plantation on the Pee Dee River. He died in March 1864 in Rome, Italy.

The daughter of a wealthy New York merchant of Irish descent, Jane Lynch Pringle was a strongly opinionated woman who possessed a somewhat domineering personality. Dr. William K. Scarborough, author of *The Allstons of Chicora Wood*, wrote of her: "She alone controlled their sons' education, planned family vacations, screened suitors, and supervised domestic affairs at the family's two plantations."[225]

Mrs. Pringle and her family were in Europe when the war broke out in 1861. Her three sons were students at Heidelberg University in Germany, and were anxious to get back to South Carolina to join the army. [226] As soon as they could, the three brothers traveled back to America at great risk. In June 1862, Mary Chesnut was in Columbia, South Carolina, and recorded in her well known diary:

---

225 Scarborough, *The Allstons of Chicora Wood*, 173.

226 A Pringle relative, William Ravenel, reported in a letter of September 1861 that Southerners trying to enter the country through northern ports were subject to arrest and imprisonment. Cote, *Mary's World*, 193.

> The sons of Mrs. John Julius Pringle have come... They seem to have had adventures enough; to get here they walked, waded, rowed in boats if boats they could find, swam rivers when boats there were none. Brave lads! One can but admire their pluck and energy. Mrs. Fisher of Philadelphia gave them money to make the attempt to get home.[227]

All three of the Pringle brothers would serve in an elite South Carolina cavalry company, the Charleston Light Dragoons.

At some point after her husband's death in 1864, Jane Lynch Pringle and her daughter Mary decided to return to America, and were back on their native soil by the fall of that year. In a memoir Mrs. Pringle wrote many years later, she stated:

> It was not easy for two women alone to travel in the autumn of 1864, but it was necessary. We had spent the four years of the war in Europe, and now a new departure had to be taken. The old regime was done and we must go home and start a new life.

Her memoir does not reveal exactly when the two women arrived in the United States, but they apparently came in through the port of New York. A relative escorted them to Norfolk, Virginia, a city occupied by Union forces, where Mrs. Pringle sought out the general in charge there and asked for his help. He questioned her:

> "Why do you want to go into the South?"
>
> I answered, to save what I could of our property.
>
> "Where are your sons?"
>
> "In Hampton's cavalry," I said.

---

227 Chesnut, *A Diary from Dixie*, 251. "Mrs. Fisher" was Eliza Izard Middleton Fisher (1815-1890), a native of South Carolina who was the wife of Joshua Francis Fisher, a prominent citizen of Philadelphia.

Married Life

"Where is your husband?"

"Dead."

The general offered to put the Pringle ladies on a special train to "the last village in the lines, after which there were forty miles of neutral territory" before they would reach Confederate lines. After a difficult and dangerous journey, Mrs. Pringle and Mary finally reached a farm in Virginia located about fifty miles from where General Wade Hampton's division, which included the Charleston Light Dragoons, was encamped. A Confederate officer who had befriended them rode to the camp to let Mrs. Pringle's son (probably Julius) know of her arrival, and he joined his mother and sister "for a few hours, after so many terrible years of separation." [228]

The memoir gives no details about how or when she and her daughter reached South Carolina, but they were back at White House Plantation as early as January 1865. Believing that they were at no greater risk there than anywhere else, Mrs. Pringle wrote to Mrs. Allston on the 15th of January:

> I try to screw Mary up to my own opinion which is to stop quietly here and try by our presence to save something, instead of going on the rampage refugeeing *where?* That's the question, shew me a safe point and I'll go tomorrow, but no such happy Valley exists in the Confederacy and I prefer the attitude of the Roman Senators when the Gauls found them sitting in their places to a sheep-like headlong flight into perhaps a worse danger and a nearer fate.[229]

---

[228] Jane Lynch Pringle's memoir, "Chaos in the South," first appeared as a newspaper article, and was later published in 1885 in *Our Women in the War*, 348-354.

[229] Easterby, *The South Carolina Rice Plantation*, 206.

Bessie in Love and War

In *Chronicles of Chicora Wood,* Bessie recorded how Jane Lynch Pringle and Mary reacted when a Union soldier named Bunker and his party of raiders arrived at White House Plantation near the end of the war:

Mrs. Pringle told us, after the Georgetown matter had been fully discussed, of her experience with the man, Bunker, who had led the negroes to Plantersville and behaved so outrageously there, turning over all the houses on the river, Chicora Wood included, to the negroes, to distribute all the contents among themselves. It was two days afterward that he came down to the White House, followed by an immense throng of negroes, and demanded wine and money. Mrs. Pringle, who was as bold as a lion and very clever, tall, stout, and of commanding presence, with the face of a man, met them on the piazza and refused to let them enter the house. Bunker had been drinking heavily and also some of the negroes. She spoke with authority, and said she knew the United States Government would not sanction the seizure of her things by a drunken mob, even though one man, the leader, had on the United States uniform; and the army regulations were severe against intoxication. She was a Northern woman herself and knew all about it, and had friends in the government and the army at that moment. Bunker was a little dashed, but very angry at being talked to in that haughty manner before his followers, and things looked ugly for a moment, so that Mary, who was standing behind her mother, began to cry, and, Bunker's attention being diverted to her, he began to try to console her. She was a very beautiful girl. He brought forward some of the things he had stolen from the Plantersville people and presented them to her—silver pitchers, etc. Mary indignantly pushed them away, but her mother bent down and said: "Take them; you can restore them to the owner." So Mary let him bring them into the piazza and present them to her, but when he tried to console her by complimentary speeches and admiring looks, she dropped her full length on the piazza in a dead faint! Mrs. Pringle took her by the feet and dragged her in through the hall to the dining-room, and, locking the door, put the key in her pocket, and returned to the mob; but they had vanished away, leaving rapidly and quietly. They no doubt, thought Mary was dead; those kind of people do not faint, and to see her brilliant, radiant color suddenly turn to deadly white and her mother drag her limp body away like that sobered them.

Knowing her future mother-in-law well, Bessie must have had some misgivings about becoming a part of her family, but she also recognized that Mrs. Pringle and her daughter Mary were capable of kindness, and that they were not without other good qualities. Mrs. Pringle loved her children deeply, and the surviving Pringle correspondence from the decade before the war is obviously that of a close-knit family. When Mrs. Pringle and Mary summered in Plantersville in 1865, Bessie remarked of them in a diary entry quoted in *Chronicles*:

> They are such an addition to this little village for, though in deep grief for the loss of Poinsett who was killed at Haw's Shop, Mrs. Pringle is so thankful to have her two other sons alive and with her that, though he was the darling of her heart, she keeps herself and her house as cheerful as possible, and does all she can to make the village brighter. Most people think it proper to be very gloomy. Of course, it is hard, all the people who were rich are now very poor but there is no good being gloomy over it. So Mrs. Pringle gives little dances now and then, and they are delightful.

Bessie in Love and War

Soon after Bessie and John Julius Pringle announced their engagement, Mrs. Allston wrote the following in a letter to Adele (who was living in Charleston):

Plantersville
27th August 1869

My dear Adele,

Before this you have received the news of Bessie's engagement. What do you think of it? I feel terribly nervous, marriage is such a solemn thing, such an awful thing. There are so many considerations of character, temper, health, ability to provide for and take care of a family &c &c. He says he has been devoted to her for five years, that he has never thought of any other woman, that he thinks he sees his way before him now, and that he believes he can make her happy. She appears very happy since, tho' she did seem very unhappy before. As I mentioned in my last, she was so irritable, so severe in everything she said, I was made miserable by it. Since the engagement she is cheerful, and I think very happy. I would have been better pleased to have seen her fate linked with a man of more animation, and intellectual elasticity, but it might be worse. She has written you how kind Mrs. P[ringle] and Mary have been. I doubt not it is a great trial to them, but they make the best of it, and have behaved with every consideration...

Mrs. Allston had always been friendly with the Pringles, but it must have displeased her when she found out that Mrs. Pringle had done all she could to delay her son's proposal to Bessie for several years. Along with her mild reservations about John Julius Pringle, this was likely one of the considerations that made Mrs. Allston "nervous" about the match, but as time wore on she became more approving of the engagement, and of her future son-in-law, whom Bessie clearly and now openly adored.

Married Life

Margaretta Pringle Childs observed that John Julius Pringle's letters to his mother, written from schools in Europe, "give proof of his active mind, warm, kindly nature, strong sense of responsibility, dramatic talent, and love of the Carolina lowcountry." Such qualities, in addition to good looks and an ardent devotion to Bessie, could not have failed to win over Mrs. Allston. In a letter dated September 12, 1869, she wrote again to Adele from Plantersville:

> You are right in concluding that I am reconciled to Bessie's engagement. She is happier than I ever saw her, and that makes me happy too. They seem perfectly devoted to each other. He appears to greater advantage than I ever saw him, being free from restraint that was formerly painful. Mrs. P and Mary have behaved with cordiality and affection, tho they give a different impression to outsiders. I suppose they think it increases their importance to seem only to endure, or to be resigned to what they can not prevent. Mrs. P said to me she had prevented it for three years, that now it is proper Julius should speak for himself, his three years hard work and economy giving assurance of his earnestness and capability.
>
> She also told me she hoped to have Bessie on her side and influence Julius thru her. She also said Bessie's music had great charms for her and was a ground of common sympathy between them. He tells Bessie his mother is delighted. If this crop proves as good, and does as much for them as they hope, they will probably be married autumn a year hence...

In another letter to Adele from Mrs. Allston dated September 30, 1869, she wrote of the newly engaged couple:

> ...Bessie is very happy. It is a pleasure to see her. Julius is as devoted as possible. He tells her he is glad she has no fortune &c. They will be married in the

spring. The latter part of April probably. This will give us a great deal of work to be gotten thru with. If the two girls go down, Arnoldus and you will be able to invite them to stay with you. Will you not? And you can assist them in shopping so much. You must consider all the things necessary.

I will give Bessie as good an outfit as I can. It will be a month before we can get any of our rice to market, but I do not wish the girls to wait for that. The sooner the work is commenced the better...

George Herbert Sass continued to write to Bessie's sister Jane after they returned to Georgetown District. In early September 1869, he remarked that he had learned of Bessie's engagement to John Julius Pringle. Although Sass mentions Bessie in several letters, he seems to have recovered as a rejected suitor by this time, but apparently, he was among at least three disappointed admirers of hers in Charleston. In a letter dated August 17, 1869, he reported to Jane that "Dr. Simons" had written to Bessie to arrange an exchange of photographs. Then, on September 20, Sass wrote: "Tell Miss Bessie that her engagement seems quite to have annihilated Manning Simons M.D. Hopes derived from the possession of photographs have vanished into thin air, and the doctor looks dyspeptic."[230]

In October 1869, Bessie made a trip to Charleston to shop for a trousseau. Still in Plantersville at this time, her mother wrote to Adele, who was hosting Bessie and Jane, "Bessie has a great deal of shopping to do. You will help her as far as you can. I wish her to get nice things and enough of them, and have them properly made and trimmed...This is to dear Bessie the great occasion of her life. I wish to spare nothing that I can afford."

Adele's diary described the "great occasion" that took place at Chicora Wood on April 26, 1870:

---

[230] Dr. Manning Simons (1846-1911), a noted Charleston physician, did not marry until late in life.

Married Life

>...Went into the country to Chicora taking with me the two little girls, to be present at Bessie's wedding, which took place on the 26th of the month. All the arrangements were very nice and successful. Bessie looked lovely in white muslin with illusion veil and orange blossoms. Julius Pringle had asked Mr. Trapier to go up and perform the ceremony which he did. Charlie gave her away. He engaged Daner for the occasion as his present to Bess, and surely it was one which gave great pleasure to all the guests.[231] Mamma looked very handsome in her black velvet and lace which she wore at our earnest solicitations, and Aunt Harrie was pretty as ever. Jane as first bridesmaid was in white with pink sash and pink flower in her hair and looked very pretty. Arnoldus came up just the day before the wedding with many other gentlemen, most of them to stay at Mrs. Pringle's. Bessie got some beautiful presents from all her friends and some of his relatives.[232]

Bessie was twenty-five at the time of her marriage, and the bridegroom was twenty-eight. They would reside at White House Plantation for most of their married life.

There are few diary entries shedding light on the six years of their marriage, but some glimpses of them can be gleaned from the letters of Mrs. Allston, who often corresponded with her daughters Adele and Jane. Family tensions were evident in a letter of August 11, 1870, when she wrote to Adele in part:

>...I think I wrote you that Mrs. Pringle said to me, Bessie dislikes Lynch so much that it will lead to something dreadful between the brothers if she does not control it. I said you are mistaken, Bessie does not dislike Lynch. She said, oh yes she does and I don't know

---

[231] This was likely a violinist, Professor James Daner, whose performances were sometimes advertised in Charleston newspapers.

[232] Adele Allston Vanderhorst's diary is found in the Vanderhorst Family Papers (SCHS).

what will come of it. I wish you would speak to Bessie and advise her. She is in a critical position. Everything that goes amiss will be attributed to her. She ought to be very discreet. I said to Mrs. P, Julius's brother and sister will always find Bessie kind and liberal in her dealings and judgment in all her conduct, and so I hope it will be ...[233]

Mrs. Pringle and her daughter Mary were away on a trip in the summer of 1870, and Bessie apparently felt happier in their absence, as Mrs. Allston implied in a letter to Adele written on September 8, 1870. She wrote, "We see Bessie every day. She is cheerful and happy. I think she has cause to dread the return of Mrs. P. and Mary, more particularly the latter, who is a jealous and mean spirited woman."

Another letter written by Mrs. Allston reveals a traumatic event that occurred at White House the following spring:

6th April 1871

My dear Adele,

...Jane wrote to you of Bessie's illness. She had a miscarriage the night of 25 or morning of 26th March. She was seriously threatened from Friday afternoon. Strange to say they did not send for the Dr. or take a step to arrest it. She was to have dined with us Saturday 25. Mary was to have driven her up. Mary came alone, brought a note from Bessie saying she had cramps in her stomach and Mrs. P[ringle] advised her not to take the drive, that Mrs. P attributed her attack to having drank a cup of milk the evening before, but she thought it the effect of cold. I and Jane invited to dine at White House the next day but the next day

---

[233] There is nothing in the published or unpublished writings of Bessie which were consulted for this book that indicate any antipathy on her part toward her brother-in-law Lynch Pringle.

Married Life

> (Sunday) it rained. We have only an open vehicle, so did not go. Monday I went. It was all over. Bessie suffered as much as one ordinarily does at a regular confinement. After having regular pains all day Saturday and Sunday at diminishing intervals, they became very severe about 12 o'clock (midnight). Mrs. P was called up to her and told me she had severe labour for three hours when all was over. It was a stormy night, which is her excuse for not calling the Dr. Bessie had after pains, and on the third day a flow of milk which was quite troublesome. It is uncertain how far advanced she was. She thought only six weeks. I never heard of these serious symptoms at such an early period. As no D[octo]r or nurse saw her thro it all, it is impossible to know certainly...

In the same letter, Mrs. Allston told Adele that Mrs. Pringle blamed her for not noticing how unwell Bessie appeared to be prior to the miscarriage:

> ...Bessie speaks with gratitude of Mrs. P.'s kindness to her. I saw her evening before last. She was still in bed, but was very cheerful. It is very disagreeable to me to go to the White House. Mrs. P. seems to me to be always in a suppressed rage, and eager to fix some blame on me, asked if I had not observed how awful Bessie had been looking, so flushed that she had expected to see her fall into an apoplectic fit. I replied, she dined with me at such a time. I noticed that she was not looking well, that her complexion was rough, that at dinner she flushed, but not so badly as I have often flushed who have been liable to it all my life, and the disagreeable and unbecoming was never regarded as alarming. She said "You are the most unobservant person I have ever seen in my life." I could only say I saw nothing unnatural in her appearance...

Bessie in Love and War

Even if a physician had been in attendance at White House that night, he could have done nothing to stop the miscarriage, although he may have been able to relieve Bessie's pain to some degree. She and her husband remained childless for the rest of their marriage. Many years later, in 1912, she wrote the following in her diary: "To think if our child had lived, he would have been forty years old and I might have had grandchildren."

It would take a long while for Bessie to recover from the miscarriage, which had weakened her health. On May 30, 1871, Mrs. Allston wrote to Adele from Plantersville:

> ...As I was walking home quite late...Lynch Pringle passed me almost at a run, saying as he passed, Julie and Bessie are in the village. They drove in just now. I saw the carry all and heard Julius. In consequence of this we walked to the Pringle's gate, but saw that the house was shut up. I then hastened home and was met by Julius on the steps and Bessie was lying on the settee. She had been taken quite ill Friday night. Saturday night she was out of her head. They had Sparkman to see her Sunday morning and he told Julius he must bring her out to me as soon as the paroxysm of fever subsided. I was indeed distressed that she should have an illness, but truly glad they had come to me. I put them in my room, and I came into your room... Sparkman saw her today and says she is better. She looks much reduced, but is very cheerful. Julius is devoted and shows to advantage...Bessie is quite free of fever tonight for the first time since Friday night...

About a month later, on June 22, 1871, Mrs. Allston informed Adele:

> ...You will probably hear from Mrs. Lynch Pringle that dear Bessie has been again quite ill, a return of the fever. When I wrote last to Jane I mentioned that she was not well. The next day she had fever and was

a week in bed. Day before yesterday she was up and down, as they say, all day. Yesterday she was up all day. It was Julius' birthday...

Writing to Adele again on March 14, 1873, Mrs. Allston reported that Bessie did not "look well. Mrs. P[ringle] is stormy and Julius is the subject of a great deal of faultfinding not to say abuse."

Mrs. Allston's letter dated August 29, 1873, recounts that Bessie and Julius spent a summer holiday on Pawley's Island with her. Mrs. Jane Pringle accompanied them to stay for a while, but when she decided to return home, she did so in anger, likely because her son and daughter-in-law were inclined to remain on the island rather than go back home with her. The letter continued:

> ...It is a week today since Mrs. Pringle left us. She said she felt perfectly well and would not consent to Julius and Bessie returning with her, saying she would not deprive Julius of his holiday, which she said would last only until the harvest began. This was quite natural and ought not to have given rise to any bad feeling, but she was in a great rage when she left, and for some days before a breakout seemed imminent. Julius went home with her and returned promptly after seeing her safely housed and servants in place...

A month later, on September 22, 1873, Mrs. Allston's letter to Adele indicated that a serious rupture had taken place in the Pringle family:

> ...You have heard from Bessie of their dreadful troubles. In her last note to me she says Mrs. Pringle has apologized and insists that she and Julius return to the White House for the winter and Bessie keep house. She goes on to say, she has consented, but Julius has not yet. I have just finished a letter to her telling her she is very <u>wrong</u>. She should never return or occupy the same house with Mrs. P. again, and never until they

take that decided stand will she feel the smallest respect for either of them. I do not wish them to act in a resentful spirit but with calm consideration for the best to all parties concerned. I do hope they will not make that arrangement. It will be fatal to Bessie's interest, intellectual, spiritual and moral. Mrs. P. is a very bad example, and imperceptibly her violence, selfishness and falseness may be [imbibed], take root, and flourish. I have seen something of the kind. It is dangerous to live with a bad example before one's eyes day out and day in for weeks and months and years. Example for good or evil is the most potent thing in life…

Bessie stated in *A Woman Rice Planter* that she spent her "very short married life" at White House (called Casa Bianca in the book), so she and her husband must have reconciled somehow with Mrs. Pringle, returning to live with her after these "dreadful troubles" in the family—if for no other reason than economic necessity.

In the spring of 1874, Mrs. Allston's letter to Adele revealed her satisfaction that Mrs. Jane Pringle would be going abroad for the summer again, giving Bessie and Julius a respite (but initiating a "time of trial" for her daughter Mary, who had married a French aristocrat in April 1873):

> Bessie passed from Friday afternoon to Tuesday afternoon with me. She was very pleasant and seemed to really enjoy the visit. We took her home Tuesday afternoon. Mrs. Pringle is going to Europe 16th of May. Her relations are so afraid of having her thrown upon them that each and all try to arrange to put the Atlantic between them. I feel for poor Mary. Her time of trial will begin when her mother joins her. They are to be in different houses, but in the same little summer resort on the seaside in N.W. of France.[234]

---

[234] This letter, written from Chicora Wood, is dated April 16, 1874.

Married Life

As revealed in the family correspondence, Bessie's relationship with her husband's family obviously had its trials and difficulties, but she loved Julius deeply, and their union was an extremely happy one. In her old age, penning her *Chronicles of Chicora Wood*, she exulted, "Never was a girl more blessed than I in her marriage, too happy to live, I often felt."

John Julius Pringle and his family faced many financial and legal troubles after the war, and they struggled to make their plantations profitable again. Despite labor problems, good crops were produced at White House Plantation, but any profits were ultimately nullified by a lawsuit for debt. In notes about the Pee Dee River plantations written by Bessie in her later years, she explained:

> After the war the eldest son John Julius planted his father's estate with his mother's counsel. There were heavy debts to be paid off and tho' he made splendid crops which sold for large sums, the necessary expenses were tremendous and by the failure of the factor to whom the crops were sent, the property became the property of Mr. James Adger and Co.[235]

In the fall of 1875, notices appeared in the Charleston *News and Courier* advertising the court-ordered disposal of White House Plantation. A lawsuit brought by James Adger and Company of Charleston resulted in a sheriff's sale of White House on November 1, 1875.

After a long pause of several years, Bessie resolved to resume her diary keeping.

Diary

Nov. 7th 1875. I have determined to write down from day to day what happens to me for my own future satisfaction. I often wish I had done so during the past

---

[235] James R. Pringle and Son, a Charleston firm, was the factor.

ten or twelve years, when so many important changes have taken place in my life that it seems to me there is nothing left to happen. We are settled married people without children. Five years of married life have passed so rapidly that I feel little older than the day I took those cares upon me. I am very far from well—over excitement about the sale of the property and overwork in the move from pineland are to blame and I hope soon to feel well again.

The legal and financial troubles that led to the loss of White House weighed heavily on Julius and Bessie. Her health suffered, and she could see that her husband's health had been worn down by hard work and his anxieties about providing for his family.

Chapter Eight:

WIDOWHOOD

BY THE SUMMER OF 1876, Bessie and Julius had taken up residence at a place she called Brookville. One of her letters of that year was addressed from "Brookville Plantation," but there are few records giving any further information on this property, which was probably located on or near the Black River in Georgetown County.[236]

The year 1876 was a pivotal one in South Carolina history, bringing the end of the carpetbagger regime. Earlier, in 1868, a new state government had been installed which was dominated by Republican carpetbaggers (outsiders), African American Republicans, and a group called scalawags (white South Carolinians who supported the Republicans). At this time South Carolina and other former Confederate states were at the mercy of their bitter enemies in Washington, the Radical Republicans, who, to ensure their control of Congress, took away the vote from men who had held office in or supported the Confederate cause. Black voters, who were mostly Republicans, were in the majority after this, and a Republican government that came to be involved

---

236 Some articles dating from the 1890s into the early 20th century in the *Georgetown Semi-Weekly Times* mention a "summer settlement" called Brooksville (rather than Brookville). A notice in that newspaper dated January 5, 1901, states that is was formerly part of Keithfield Plantation, and identifies it as "being the house and premises formerly occupied by the late John Julius Pringle." The property was later owned by Mrs. Esther J. Sampson. A rental advertisement for a "summer house" at Brooksville, placed by J.L. LaBruce, appeared in the *Georgetown Sunday Outlook* on March 23, 1902.

in extensive corruption took over the state.[237] The disenfranchised white Democratic voters eventually regained their right to vote, but the corrupt carpetbagger rule continued until November 1876, when Wade Hampton, a former Confederate general, was elected governor of South Carolina. The campaign that preceded his election was a tumultuous, desperate one, as the Republicans sought to preserve their control of the state government, and the white Democrats, along with some black Democrats, struggled to win enough votes to oust the Republicans.

In mid-August 1876, John Julius Pringle left home to attend the South Carolina Democratic Party convention at the state capital, Columbia.[238] As revealed in a letter written by his mother-in-law Mrs. Allston, she accompanied him on his journey as far as Charleston, where they paid a visit to her daughter Adele Vanderhorst. He stayed one night at the Vanderhorst home, and then left the next morning for Columbia. Mrs. Allston recalled in her letter, "He seemed well, was as kind, respectful and attentive to me as a son. He left us next morning after breakfast. My last word to him was pray take care of yourself. He replied, I will."[239]

The convention in Columbia began on August 15 and ended on August 17. John Julius Pringle returned to Charleston after the event, and at some point just before or during his stop there, he fell ill. He died on August 21, 1876.

This clipping of an undated newspaper notice was found in Bessie's diary of 1876:

---

[237] "The Reconstruction government was corrupt at all levels and was responsible for stealing millions of dollars from the citizens of South Carolina by perpetuating all types of financial scams ... The majority of the money ended up in the pockets of members of the Reconstruction government and their friends." Shull, *A Guidebook of Southern States Currency*, 297-298.

[238] At this convention, which met August 15 through August 17, 1876, the state Democratic Party put forth its platform and nominated Wade Hampton as the gubernatorial candidate.

[239] This letter from Mrs. Allston to Bessie is dated August 31, 1876. Bessie had written to her mother to ask about her last experiences and conversations with John Julius Pringle.

DEATH OF MR. JOHN JULIUS PRINGLE

The death of this estimable young gentleman, which occurred suddenly in Charleston on the 21st inst., was a heavy stroke, and rendered intensely so by its being sudden and unlooked for. Mr. Pringle left here a very short while ago to attend the State Democratic Convention at Columbia, in the prime and vigor of health and manhood; and so sudden was the termination of his life, that his family was denied the privilege of ministering to his last moments. Mr. Pringle was young, being only in the thirty fifth year of his age, and full of promise; he was a cultivated gentleman, of genial and kind manners, full of honor and integrity, and entertained liberal views backed by an excellent judgment. He though a quiet and unassuming gentleman never swerved from public duty whenever imposed upon him, but took pleasure in answering the calls made by those who delighted to honor him.

The whole community who sincerely and deeply deplore his early death, feel the deepest sympathy for his afflicted family.

The death certificate of John Julius Pringle, signed by Dr. John L. Dawson, gave the cause of death as malarial fever. His funeral services were held at St. Michael's Episcopal Church in Charleston on August 23, 1876.

Shortly before his death, Bessie's mother, who had been unwell, had left Charleston to spend some time in Flat Rock for her health. When the news of his passing reached her, Mrs. Allston wrote feelingly to her bereaved daughter:

Bessie in Love and War

25 August 1876
Farmers Hotel, Flat Rock, N.C.

My darling Bessie,

My beloved daughter, my heart is with you. My arms and home are wide open to you. May God strengthen, sustain and comfort you as He only can. I am dumb and open not my mouth for He has done it.

I wish I were with you. I will join you as soon as I can.

Pray try to keep up. Do not give way to murmuring or despair but try to put your trust in God and as a little child subject to His will. May He help you and give you the light of remembrance is the earnest prayer of your devotedly attached.

Mamma

Bessie was on Pawley's Island with her brother Charles when she learned of her husband's illness. Her cousin James Petigru Lesesne came to bring the urgent news and take her to Charleston, but John Julius Pringle was already dead by the time she left. He had passed away at 5 Legare Street, the Charleston home of Arnoldus and Adele Vanderhorst, and his body was placed in an "ice coffin" there. This excerpt from a letter by Bessie's brother Charles gives details of those tragic hours:

Plantersville
Aug. 27th 1876

Dear Mamma,

Brother received a letter from you this morning. You had just heard of Julius's illness. Jim arrived at the island yesterday week ago about 3 o'clock. We had been looking for Julius since Saturday night and when I heard an exclamation from Jim and a man's step I made sure it was he but when I looked round and recognized Jim my heart stood still. I literally could not speak for some seconds but never thought of Julius being ill until he spoke. It really came like a "thief in the night." From Jim's account to me I had very little or no hope, but it came to Bessie very gradually and not until that night at Brookville did she know how serious I thought it. She held up wonderfully well. I [intended] going down with her but did not tell her so, just went on from one place to the next as though about to turn back so as not to alarm her too much, but when I woke up before daylight at Brookville I found that I could not travel. I had one of those giddy turns with nausea that just made it impossible. They got off in very good time and I then went to bed again and slept soundly, got up about 8 and went back to Chicora and over to the beach, Brother going with me to the island. The next day, Wednesday, about 1o'clock I got a note from Jim at Kingstree sent by the carriage. They had met the [northbound] train and heard of his death and it was impossible to keep it from Bess. She behaved remarkably well. By the st[eame]r that evening I heard again from Jim. Julius had been put in an ice coffin so that Bessie saw him without disfiguration and as Jim said he looked very noble in death.[240] Mrs. Mason Smith and Bessie stayed at the house that night and he was buried the next day. Bessie had a small lot bought at Magnolia for the purpose...

A letter written by Bessie's Aunt Harry (Harriette Petigru Lesesne) to Mrs. Allston on September 5, 1876, describes the funeral, Bessie's behavior, and her return to Brookville:

My dear Sister,

I rec[ieve]d yours of the 28th Aug[us]t, was glad to find you had rec[ieve]d both my letters. You seem

---

240 There were different types of "ice coffins" in use in the latter part of the 19th century. They were typically a wooden casket insulated by ice, with a glass window through which the deceased's face could be seen.

anxious to know about dear Bessie's plans, of course you have heard from Jane all about them. Dear Jane came down in the Saturday boat of the 26th of Aug[us]t. Julius was buried Wednesday afternoon the 23rd Aug[us]t. Dear Bessie came home with me from the cemetery. She stood by the grave till every clod of earth was put in it, smoothed over and leveled, and oh how long it seems to take! She was perfectly calm, and she then rec[ieve]d the crowns, and wreaths and crapes of flowers from the hands of the pallbearers, and placed them carefully upon the grave, with an absorbed look as if not conscious of anyone's presence. James was in attendance upon her. She then calmly got into the carriage, gave way to no violent grief. She went to her room on getting home, laid on the sofa, said very little. James came in to see her, she talked to him a good deal. He would not leave till he saw her quietly in bed. She slept very well that night, the next night not so well.

She said she felt as if nothing was real, as if she was out of the body, and looking on at something happening to someone else. She scarcely wept till she saw Lynch Pringle, who arrived the day after. Jane's coming was a great comfort or help. She was very sad, but behaved with so much good sense. Bessie's whole being seemed filled with the spirit of charity and submission to the will of God, and I think the grace of God rested upon her and gave her strength not her own. She has shown wonderful strength of character and fortitude. There was no repining nor bewailing herself, no bitterness. I observed that it seemed to distress her to hear an unkind word of anyone.

She visited his grave every afternoon during her stay in town. Jane told me that she seemed more cheerful as soon as she entered the cemetery. Quantities of flowers were sent her, which she carried every afternoon and laid on his grave. She feels confident that

Widowhood

he has entered into rest, and she seems only to desire to follow him when it may please God to take her. His relatives were devoted to her. She rec[eive]d all that sympathy and aff[ection]ate attention could do to alleviate her sorrow. She saw her friends in her room, and in the ev[eni]ng in the upper piazza, where she had a cool breeze. Jane and herself left in the boat of Wednesday the 30th. I have heard from Jane. They had an unusually quick and comfortable trip. They reached Brookville at half past three o'clock. Bessie preferred going back there, and she has a Miss Ford to stay with her. Lynch Pringle went back with them. Jane says she will go as often as possible to see dear Bessie, and so will Charles. Jane says Bessie is more satisfied there than she could be elsewhere...

From Brookville, Bessie wrote again to her mother, who was still in Flat Rock.

5 September [1876]
Brookville Plantation

Thank you, dear Mamma, for y[ou]r long letter just received. I have so longed to hear some detail about July from the time he left me. It seemed so hard that others should have heard all his last words tho' he was entirely unconscious that they were last words. I cannot find that he mentioned my name at all tho' I know how he must have longed for me, except Saturday evening when Mrs. W[illia]m Bull Pringle who had not been out of the house for 8 weeks before went round to see him and said she would write to me but he said 'oh no that would frighten her and isn't necessary for I will write myself in the morning.'[241] When the morning came tho' expressing himself as so much better and the

---

241   Mrs. William Bull Pringle was Mary Motte Alston Pringle (1801-1884), who lived on King Street in Charleston (in a house now known as the Miles Brewton House).

Doctor saying to him y[ou]r fever is gone entirely and if you take care of y[ou]rself you'll be all right directly, he did not write. The Doctor told him to remain in bed and you know writing in bed is very inconvenient, but oh I suppose you have heard it all and I will not, cannot go over it—the fearful feeling that if I had been there, I might have seen and felt the change coming and done something to stave it off will fill my heart with bitter regret and yearning that I should not have been with my darling when he wanted me.

Mr. Barker and [Mother] Pringle were with him.[242] Mr. B. told me that he shewed an indisposition to talk to them but lay quiet with his eyes closed and oh I know he was longing to have me by him as he heard the bells ringing for church and thought of our little home service every Sunday. Oh it seems too cruel, too cruel that there was nothing to tell me that Sunday as we drove to Church on the beach and sat thru the service unmoved that all that made life bright and dear to me was fading out so quickly and so surely.

When we went into church he was almost well and when we came out he was unconscious of all earthly sights or sounds. Oh my God, and I went into church nervous, agitated and came out in excellent spirits for the first time since we had been on the beach. The hymns were 'Lord forever at thy side' and 'Am I a soldier of the Cross.' Sometimes I think that if I had been able to give my whole heart to God during that service as it is sometimes given us to do my darling might have been spared to me.

That night we went to church at the parsonage and the service was very comforting and earnest.[243] We

---

242   This was likely Theodore Gaillard Barker, a Charleston lawyer and friend of the family.
243   The parsonage of All Saints Episcopal Church was located on Pawleys Island. It was not unusual for summer services to be held there.

sang 'How firm a foundation' and when we walked home we sat ever so long on the sand hills and gazed at the night, the stars very bright but just overhead a singular black cloud, very black, only one and we talked about it. I said it looked like a ship in full sail. Charley said it looked like a huge black monster. Nothing told me it was over me that it hung so threateningly, nothing warned me to pray with agony for my absent one who lay so still between life and death just hovering. I think it would have killed me and I was wicked enough to long for death until I saw him.

Oh Mamma, how I wish you could have seen him. I had made James promise that if he were above ground I should see him, but when we got to town others interfered to me from him, [but] I asserted my right and said you have all been with him and had the privilege of nursing him which has been denied me but now he is mine and I will see him. So they let me go, and oh the relief, the comfort, as I lifted the blanket which covered the temporary coffin and gazed down through the glass. My whole being broke into a smile and I murmured 'oh death where is thy sting.' He was beautiful with a beauty not of this world. A look of supreme happiness and peace such as I have never seen on his face in life. My darling, my darling as he always soothed and comforted me in life and comforted me in death. I felt it would be an insult to him to cry and mourn in his presence.

But then they said I must not stay there but go round to Aunt Harry's. I plead [sic] and begged but my great wish was to do right as he would have wished and when Mrs. Wm. B. Pringle and Aunt H. said I ought to go I yielded, but Annie Wells had heard me begging and she took them aside and said her mother would come and stay with me and that no one could say anything to that and before I heard anything more of it Mrs. S came and she was such a comfort.[244] She let me stay in the next room with the folding doors open and go in just as often as I wished to look at him and she repeated hymn after hymn which was all I cared for and begged me to sleep so that I might do all my last duties to him calmly, so I slept three times during that last night I spent on earth with him and a great calm came over me. Whenever I began to give way I went in and gazed at him until I was calm again. The two sentences which ran through my head incessantly were "Blessed are the pure in heart for they shall see God." Little Fanny is not purer in heart than he was.[245] "Blessed are the merciful for they shall receive mercy." He was tender and merciful to what seemed to worldly eyes a fault. Oh Mamma, God has been merciful to me in making me feel such an assurance of his safety through the mercy of our Saviour, expressed in those words which apply so well to him.

As long as I can think of him free from all his long labor, all care, anxiety, weariness, suffering, I keep calm, but when I look at my poor self I break down completely. The years ahead look so dark. I feel utterly without interest in any earthly thing. Everyone seemed shocked when they asked me first where I would go. I said Brookville, but as I never varied and could not bear the thought of anything else, they kindly let me have my own way. Someone said something about its not being proper. That was a terrible blow and shock but I said there are many excellent ladies who would gladly come to me for a small sum. Someone asked me who and I just answered at random a Miss Eliza Ford

---

244 Annie Wells was likely Anna Mason Smith Wells (1850-1924), whose husband was Edward Laight Wells (1839-1917). "Mrs. S" was probably Anna Wells' mother, Eliza Middleton Huger Smith (1824-1919). The Smith and Pringle families were related.

245 Fanny was likely Bessie's niece Frances Allston Vanderhorst, who was born in 1873.

WIDOWHOOD

who's [sic] hair is quite grey which seemed satisfactory.[246] As far as I was concerned it was accidental but I believe it was providential. She came as soon as I wrote to her. Is helping me make up my clothes and is very helpful and excellent. She reads or repeats hymns to me at night until sleep comes and then slips back to her own room.

Dear Jinty seemed hurt at first that I wouldn't consent to her staying, but you know Mamma I could not keep her any longer from the children and I could not consent to the children who are so delicate making the change down here. She comes to see me almost every other day and it is a great comfort. I hope you understand about it. She can be so much to the children and no one can really do me any good now but God.[247] My earthly support has been taken away and I must beware of clinging to any other on earth and strive only to learn the support held out from above. Here in this house I can never feel lonely as long as God gives me that wonderful feeling of nearness to Him. I am only afraid of losing it.

My dear Mamma I must stop for it is after ten and I feel very tired. Give my love to dear Della and kiss all the children specially little [Tim] and beg little Adele to write to me and big Adele too.[248] I look for the mail eagerly hoping always I may hear some new scrap about him during that week. Kiss dear little Julia for me, you know how fond July was of her and my namesake and

---

246 This may be an Elizabeth C. Ford, who is listed in the 1870 South Carolina census as a teacher, age 45, in Georgetown, S.C.

247 Bessie's younger sister Jane (Jinty) was helping to take care of the children of her brother Benjamin, whose wife Ellen had passed away in 1875.

248 Bessie is referring to her sister Adele Vanderhorst, and her niece Adele Vanderhorst, who was born in 1865.

Poinsett when you see him.²⁴⁹ How I hope the new baby will look like July.

Goodbye dear Mamma. Write to me often and try and get strong and well so as to help me on thro' the long years ahead.

Yr devoted daughter Bessy

Bessie received many touching letters of condolence from family and friends in the weeks following her husband's death. During this time, she continued to stay at Brookville. This excerpt from a letter from Bessie's sister Jane to their mother Mrs. Allston, offers a glimpse of her life there as a widow:

Plantersville
Sept. 10th [1876]
Sunday

Dear Mama,

I have not heard from you for such an age. I think letters seem to take longer to get to and from Flat Rock than they do ordinarily here. I have just got back from Brookville. Charlie and I went down after church. I had intended to have very early dinner and go down after but Eliza Ford came over to church and told me that Bessie confidently expected us and would wait dinner for us so we came home and got in the buggy immediately. It does look so sad to see her sitting in the piazza, in her deep black and little old lady's widow's cap. It makes her look so unlike her old self. She is calm and at times one might almost say content, but of course she has her very bitter moments. The effort she has made for calm and resignation seems to me almost super human, and I know it can only be through a higher power working within her that it is attained.

---

249 Bessie's brother Charles had a daughter named Julia, born in January 1876.

Widowhood

I suppose Aunt Harriet wrote you how wonderful her behavior during the first terrible days was. I never would have supposed it possible for one of her temperament to receive a blow such as this was in the way she did. James told me that after the first few moments at Kingstree when it came with such cruel suddenness, that he had never seen anything like her self control. One may imagine what hours of agony these [were].

She had to pass there and fortunately she had put her prayer book in her bag and she told me she took it out on the train and read the burial service through and from that moment felt perfectly calm. Her anguish was increased by the thought that each moment [rendered] the chance of her seeing him again for the last time on earth less likely. It was a great mercy that she did not see him, it would have been very different with her if she had done. It seems the greatest comfort she has now to think of him as he was after death with a sweet, peaceful, happy expression on his face and they all say such a noble look…

Knowing that her mother was worried about her and wishing to be with her, Bessie wrote to Mrs. Allston again later in September:

19 September 1876
Brookville

Dear Mamma,

Your sweet letter was a great comfort to me, tho' I feel truly distressed at Elias' illness.[250] Dear Dell, it is very hard on her going away for the health and benefit of the whole family, to have so much sickness and nursing and anxiety. Please kiss the dear child for me and tell her I will write to her soon and that I have thought of her a great deal since I got y[ou]r letter.

---

250 This was Adele's son, Elias Vanderhorst (1869-1937).

Neither of you need be anxious about me for I am well and take all the necessary precautions against sickness. I feel that it would [sic] a terrible thing for poor Jinty to have me taken sick now and so I am very careful.

Jinty was down here today and said they were all well in the village, that is at home, but there has been a good deal of fever among the villagers generally. Dr. Sparkman and then [Thorne] and then Mr. George Ford all quite ill with fever.[251] I think a good deal had been said to frighten Miss Ford about this place and I do hope the good soul may escape any indisposition while here.

Brother passed through about nine this morning on his way to the grange at White's Bridge, said he might come back and spend the night. Poor Mr. Richardson received news this evening of the death of his mother in Savannah of yellow fever or at least the servant told us so when he brought the mail.[252] His poor mother has been a fearful invalid and suffered for so many years, and to die at last of a terrible epidemic seems sad. When her daughter Mary was nursing her alone, all the servants in the yard had yellow fever, and Mr. Richardson unable to go to her assistance. All this Lynch told me last night. Of course I have not seen Mr. R[ichardson]. Lynch is very kind and attentive in every way having grass cut for the cows etc. etc. I have begged Charly to try and sell the cows one by one but as yet have not been called on for them.

It is terribly sad to me to break up my house altogether but there is nothing else to be done and it does

---

251 This may have been George Gaillard Ford (1829-1900), a son of George Thomas Ford (1806-1869).

252 This was likely John Richardson (1845-1920), a resident of Plantersville and a native of Georgia. His mother, Elizabeth Phoebe Stoney Richardson, died on September 15, 1876.

not seem to me that I could live anywhere else in the country up here I mean. Brother kindly begged me to make my home with him and that seems the right thing for me to do perhaps, but as yet I cannot make up my mind to it. The responsibility of children I am not certain of being equal to and then I always look to his marrying again. I don't think a single life suits him. I gave him no definite answer.

My great desire is to do what would have pleased July most, and by his kind thoughtfulness I will not be left penniless I would like best to establish a home for myself however small, as the thing he would have liked best. When I say <u>home</u> I mean renting rooms or a very small house or anything which would enable me to have some of his home things around me, his gun and his dog [Sandy]. I think you will understand what I mean.

Arnoldus and Brother have both been most kind and perhaps my views will be modified after a time. My present wish is to be near <u>him</u>. I can make no plans until I talk with you for your opinion will guide me almost entirely. July had great confidence in y[ou]r judgment and so have I.

I think there is very little doubt that Mrs. Pringle will come out at once if the blow has not killed her. Her letters to July have come thick and fast and I know her to be <u>utterly</u> unprepared for such terrible tidings. Five have come from Mary and herself since his death. One from Mary came last night full of affection saying she had sent me a p[ai]r of corsets which were of the best make but too small for her.

In the event of Mrs. Pringle's coming I would like to have all my plans decided beforehand for she is very fond of arranging things for other people, so do dear Mamma think of the matter seriously. I think Jinty will probably leave you before long and tho' I am in no way fitted to take her place you and I could be together and have brother's children. All plans must necessarily be indefinite in the present condition of the country, and it is dreadful to me to look at the future at all, but that idea gives me less pain than any other and if we could get a very small house with a large yard for the children to play in, it might be feasible it seems to me, but as I said before I will be governed almost entirely by you in the matter.

Dear Mamma you must not say you did not show your affection for and appreciation of July. You were always sweet to him, and he was very fond of you and always very pleased to win your approval. I don't think many knew how much earnestness there was in his character. To me he was everything that it is possible for one mortal to be to another and his tenderness to me this summer was wonderful. "My little War Bessie" he called me constantly, and went over twice this summer, the last time two days before he left home, all the details of our meeting at Kingstree in 62 and traced our friendship from that time up, and thanking me for being such a good wife to him.[253] My darling gave me credit for a great deal which was only the natural development of his own noble nature. On the beach those days we were alone, when I was nervous and fretful and anxious and strangely unstrung he sat at home with me all the time and would say every now and then "My child I don't know what makes me love you so."

I thank God from my heart for the seven years of great happiness which He gave us, and I feel very much as I used to think people must feel whose husbands had to leave them to spend a summer in Europe, only that I have no anxiety about him. Sometimes it seems impossible to get over the day. I miss him so and then

---

253 Bessie first met John Julius Pringle on a railroad trip to Charleston in November 1862, so he may have boarded the train at Kingstree, S.C.

Widowhood

I pray for patience and to feel that it is after all only for a little while that we are separated. And then when things arise which would have worried and harassed him it is such a comfort to know that he is beyond them now. Last week the rain poured down for three days and when I lay awake at night and heard it and knew how much rice was on the [stubble] and how he would have worried over it, and then all the labor trouble. Oh I know it is better for him.

He shewed very little of what he felt but he suffered a great deal, and I yearn over his life of labor and anxiety and mortification for the past three or four years. If he had had the smallest competency without debt, he would have lived to be an old man in all human probability.

I hope Caroline's little boy who is named after him may have his character and disposition.[254] As he is not my Godchild, I can hope to have no possible influence over him, but blood is a wonderful thing and he may grow up gentle and sweet just like July for all we know. I hope he will not have outgrown the likeness to him which you mention before I see him. Caroline wrote me a very sweet letter as did [Fannie]. Please thank them both and say I will write as soon as I can.

Miss Ford continues satisfactory. Poor soul she has had a joyless life with much sorrow, care and hard work and consequently has a very real and grateful sense of the transitoriness of this life. Now dear Mamma goodnight. Write to me. I look eagerly for letters.

Kiss the dear children for me beginning with Adele straight through and Fan and Bessie twice.[255] Kiss little

---

254 Bessie's sister-in-law Caroline Lowndes Pringle (1846-1919), the wife of Dominic Lynch Pringle, had a son named John Julius Pringle who was born in 1876.

255 Fan and Bessie were Adele Vanderhorst's daughters Frances (born 1873), and Elizabeth (born 1871).

Julia when you see her and Poinsett.²⁵⁶ I inherit his godchildren so I have 12, six of my own and six of his. Kiss Della for me and tell her I will write as soon as I can. I think of both of you constantly and pray that Elias is better.

Yr devoted daughter
E.W. Pringle

In September 1876, about a month after her husband's death, Bessie resumed her diary, beginning the first entry with scripture verses:

"Blessed are the pure in heart for they shall see God."

"Blessed are the merciful for they shall receive mercy."

Thank God for these words of our blessed Saviour.

"Ah if you knew what peace there is in an <u>accepted</u> sorrow." My Father give me that peace which passes all understanding. My darling has been taken and I thank Thee oh God for the mercy which has made me feel that he is safe thro' our Saviour and now I pray for strength for my poor self that I may be guided always and entirely by Thy spirit in my loneliness and perplexity. Many, many things have made me feel my darling has been taken from evil to come. He suffered no one can tell how acutely from the circumstances which surrounded him—debt, complications of law questions etc. etc.—he felt keenly, and his eagerness to succeed in paying off the debt which weighed upon him, his hard labor with a view to that, day after day in the scorching sun and then in the evening paying off in the close store surrounded by negroes. Oh my darling, my darling I yearn over y[ou]r life of labor and anxiety.

---

256 Poinsett was a son of Caroline and Dominic Lynch Pringle. His full name was Joel Roberts Poinsett Pringle (1873-1932).

WIDOWHOOD

It is a little more than a month since I parted from him and it seems as the years ahead had dragged themselves between. My great wish is to act in every way as he would have had me do and it is so difficult to know what he would have wished about every little matter. Already little things have made me understand how difficult it will be to satisfy everyone. My darling had two guns and a rifle (besides his rifle club rifle). In speaking to his brother I asked him if there was anything he wanted to [take home] and I should gladly give it to him. He said he would like his Father's gun which July had. I said certainly. He then asked me something about the other gun and I said it was here in the store room just where my dear husband had laid it. He said I had better let him take it and have it cleaned and put up so I went to the store room and with tears saw it moved from the spot where he had it Saturday Aug. 12th when he brought it from the beach.

Today L[ynch] was here and said something about wishing me to gather up all the little things which belonged to the gun to have put up in the case and I said please have the box made as light as possible so that I can have it moved about with me. He looked so shocked and surprised that I have been quite agitated ever since for fear I have been unreasonable. I had said to him before I shall keep the gun for one of y[ou]r little boys, and intend it to belong to Poinsett but I would like until he is old enough to keep it myself. I would have it cleaned from time to time by a gunsmith. It was my darling's constant companion. He rarely moved without one or the other. The breechloader he had made in Baltimore four years ago and was particularly fond of and so I was glad when Lynch said he would like to have the other which was his father's, a Perdy which

July thought all the world of.[257] L. has himself a very fine breechloader and I scarcely think he could use and keep nice three guns.

Oh my precious, if you only had known what was coming and had written down what you wanted done with all y[ou]r little things. My only pleasure now is to carry out y[ou]r wishes but it is so hard to know what to do. I know you loved me more than anyone else and y[ou]r little personal things which are so precious to me to others only go by their intrinsic value.

Oh if the hope which I had at first when grief dried up the sources of nature had been realized then there would have been someone else to whom every relic of you would have been dear. God knows best. Be still my heart and trust Him. Oh it is hard not to long and wish for a child of his blood to cherish and do for. My July my baby God knows how good you were to me, how kind and gentle and patient, and when you were weak how you let me help you, and oh it is so precious to me to think how for the last two months your love seemed to grow stronger and stronger, how you said constantly 'My darling I don't know what makes me love you so.' 'My wife my wife who has helped me so' and then he called me constantly 'My little [dear] Bessie' and more than once he put his head on my lap kneeling before me and said 'My darling I pray God to make me good and strong for your sake.' And I said 'no darling for Christ's sake' and he acquiesced in the change.

I got this morning a postal card written by him Wednesday Aug. 16th and the last words are "I have steadily remembered something." Oh my darling I thank you for those parting words. I had said on parting 'Be good' and other entreaties to him to keep himself

---

257 This was likely a breechloader shotgun made by British gunmakers James Purdey and Sons.

strong. My own heart, no woman ever was blessed with a purer more perfect love than I have been and I thank God for it with all my heart. Writing this is such a relief to me, I cannot talk to anyone as I can write knowing it is for no human eye. I feel as if was writing to my beloved.

Mr. Wells wrote a kind note to L. speaking of the [dogs] which were being broken and saying if I wished to withdraw [them] no expense had as yet been incurred and to let him know where to have them sent. It was a great relief for I thought $55 would have to be paid on them, so I wrote a few lines and begged him to accept 'Scot' and send 'Chips' back to me. I feel quite sure in that I did what you would wish. Sandy I want to keep and Chips and the newer hound I shall give away to someone you would have liked to have them.

The future is still perfectly unsettled. I feel sure you would have wished me to have a home of my own however small and I shall try and accomplish that thanks to y[ou]r forethought, in spite of my opposition. Cousin [J] a kind old gentleman sent me $100 which relieved me of much anxiety as to the funeral expenses which I wished to bear entirely myself.[258] The bills for my mourning are still due but they can wait awhile. I paid this morning the bill for y[ou]r last shirts to Mrs. Anderson. Oh my child y[ou]r trousseau as you called it has come and I expect by every [batch] yet the little valise from Mr. H. He wrote a most kind note speaking of you as having been more than a friend to him.

I wonder darling if it is wrong to write in this way. I shouldn't think so but I feel sure if it is wrong God will make me feel it. He has been so good and soothed and comforted me so. I dreamed of you last night. It was so

---

258 This may have been her cousin John Earl Allston, who had gifted Bessie's mother $5000 in 1869.

sweet to be with you again, but somehow a [rafter] broke in the house and I woke in great agitation. My baby I miss you so. When I am weak and suffering you were always so sweet to me then, and my back has seemed as broken as my heart for the last few days. Lily made me a pine gum plaster which I think does me a little good. Now it is dusk and I must stop.

Tuesday Sept. 19th. Written to Mamma to ask her to consider my future and give me her advice, for it will be governed very much by her opinion. July had great confidence in her judgment and so have I.

L. was with me a long time before Jane and Charley came Sunday and I told him if he would rather keep the breechloader he was welcome to do so only I wanted to keep one with me and wanted that gun to belong to Poinsett. He seemed much relieved and said he would prefer to keep that. I must try and not be unreasonable. The things are sacred in my eyes, but I must not expect that to be the case with everyone. My darling I have tried hard to be good and patient and God has helped me and made me feel all his mercies. It is a month today since you dressed for the last time. I wish so I knew what clothes you put on that I might kiss them and pat them. I think it was the blue flannel coat Miss Ford made you for in the pocket to that I found several papers and the two postals I had directed to you. And now precious goodnight.

Last night a letter from Mary to July, they had not yet heard. Oh I feel so sorry for them. It is dreadful to read letters written all unconscious of the terrible blow hanging over them.

Sept. 21st. One month today since my beloved passed from this life, I trust to one far happier. It is dreadful to be getting daily farther from my last look at his loved face. Oh my darling I pray God to make me feel instead

Widowhood

that I am one day nearer to our meeting in Heaven, and what is an earthly parting compared to a heavenly meeting. If I can only keep it in my mind and strive every second to live so that I may be meet for that day.

I got yesterday evening the valise containing the suits sent for by my darling to Bird and Co. and brought out by Mr. Hill. Oh my child, my child it is heartrending to think with what pleasure we would have opened them together, and now I don't know what to do about them. I don't think you would have liked them precious. They are very loud except the coat and the suit. Then your gloves and my gloves and my waterproof, your last present. Oh my beloved, how can I get through the many days and weeks and months without you. Only God's grace in making me keep my eyes fixed upon Heaven can enable me to get through them.

Last night Lynch sent me over a little package which came in a box to him from Dinard, a present from Mary, a pretty pair of corsets and some [yards] of Breton lace and a neat neck ornament of velvet.[259] It was very sweet of her to send them. She has always been very good to me, tho' it was hard for her, being so fond of you, to see you marry and look for your happiness [in] someone else. I cannot keep my mind from Dinard. I know the blow will fall so heavily on both Mary and her mother. Lynch got a letter from the latter announcing as great good news that [illegible name] had gone with his Mother to Orleans to be formally adopted by his uncle Jules [M.] Polinac! To take his title and be his heir which I suppose is only a name. So that I really don't know what Mary's rightful address is. Whatever

---

259 Bessie's mother-in-law and sister-in-law were in Dinard, a town on the coast of Brittany in France. Bessie's sister-in-law Mary Izard Pringle was the wife of Yvan Marie Edmond Colas des Francs. He was the son of Albert Colas des Francs and Louise Constance Isaure de Polignac. The uncle "Polinac" referred to may be the brother of Louise Constance Isaure de Polignac, Julien Alexandre Constantin de Polignac (born 1817).

it is I shall always love her and feel tenderly for her, for July and herself were very fond of each other.

I have spent all day reading over Mrs. Pringle's letters for a year passed [sic]. They are as good as a journal of the time for they recall so much to mind. They are very clever and show a wonderful mind and foresight. She always said she was a Cassandra.

Yesterday I spent all the morning at the W[hite] House putting my darling's desk in order, but I am so weak that I accomplished very little and have suffered for that little ever since. My back aches so. I put his dear great coat which is associated with him out to sun and when I went to take it in, Sandy was lying on it and gave one long piteous howl as I took it off the railing of the little platform. It went to my heart. Every thing loved him and even the dumb things miss him sadly.

In early October, Bessie penned a letter to her mother-in-law Mrs. Pringle, who by then had learned of the death of her son John Julius Pringle. The following excerpt reveals her continuing grief, and the reasons she left Brookville:

Plantersville
October 2nd 1876

Dear Mrs. Pringle,

...[N]ow that he is gone the tenderness of love of those he loved is everything to me. My burden often feels too heavy for me to stagger under and did God not in his mercy help me to look up and think of his release from labor and care I should lose my mind...I have been obliged to leave Brookville for there with his dressing room just as he left it, his big tub and sponge, and [dear] shabby working clothes hanging round—his pipe and tobacco all about the dining room where he left them, I felt so near to him, as tho' the veil was very

WIDOWHOOD

thin that concealed him from me—and then I felt as tho' I could help Lynch a little and relieve the sense of loneliness, but Miss Ford whom I got to stay there and keep house and sew for me was taken sick and was so frightened that I had to send her home, and then Lynch and Jane and Charley would not consent to my remaining there alone...

Diary

Oct. 13th. It is two months since I passed my last day with my darling, and thank God it was such a blessed happy day. It was Sunday, and we drank a bottle of champagne in honor of the 22nd August wh[ich] was the 7th anniversary of our engagement. I suggested it saying w[oul]d not be together on that day and he was pleased to do it tho' he assured me he w[oul]d be back by that time and we would be together, and we were together for I reached Charleston and I saw his blessed face in its last peaceful sleep on the evening of the 22nd Tuesday about 8 o'clock. Oh God I pray thee keep me pure and good and help me with Thy Grace, so that I may not give way to morbid bitter thoughts but trust in Thee. Oh my darling, my darling I miss you so.

In a letter written in October 1876, Bessie asked Mrs. Luquer, an acquaintance and relative by marriage, for a photograph of her late husband.[260]

Dear Mrs. Luquer,

You will no doubt be surprised to see my handwriting and I hope you will forgive my bothering you. I wish

---

260 The Luquer family of New York was related to the Lynch and Pringle families. In Bessie's later correspondence, there is a letter to her from Eloise P. Luquer, who writes to her as a cousin. This was likely Eloise Payne Luquer (1862-1947) of Bedford, N.Y. The Mrs. Luquer to whom the 1876 letter is addressed may have been Eloise's mother, Eloise Elizabeth Payne Luquer (1834-1894), or her aunt, Sarah Lea Lynch Luquer (1809-1887).

to ask you a favor. I want you to take the photograph you have of July to [Hartz] and have him to make a large one and send it to me by mail with the bill. I do not wish it colored.

It is just two months today since I last saw my beloved husband in life and it seems as tho' years had passed in between us. I have but one small photograph of him and tho' that is excellent I long so for something more. Life seems so utterly empty and desolate for me that tho' from my heart I say Thy will be done I find it impossible to rouse myself to an interest in anything or to face the future wh[ich] stretches out before me like a dreary desert wh[ich] has to be traversed before I can see his blessed face again.

My only excuse for troubling you is the affection with which I have always heard July speak of you and of your kindness to him as a boy. He spoke with such pleasure of seeing you this month when he intended to spend a few weeks at the north. With love to your daughters, I am my dear Mrs. Luquer yours affect[ionatel]y

Elizabeth W. Pringle

While living in Plantersville, Bessie contemplated her future. She would soon take a short trip to Charleston, but she was unsure about where she would spend the winter—and the rest of her life—as this excerpt from one of her letters discloses:

Plantersville
Oct. 21st 1876

Dearest Mama,

I feel reproached for not having written to you before, but it is very hard for me to write composedly much more so than to talk. Every day makes me feel my loss more and more and there is never a waking

Widowhood

moment when July is not in my thoughts, even when I am talking to others on trivial subjects. It is two months today since he breathed his last, and it seems as tho' years had passed. You are very kind in wishing me to stay at Chicora this winter. When you come down we will see about it. I would not need more than one room as I should leave what few things I have at the White House locked up in one room until I decide on something permanent. As far as I can see now I will stay with Brother this winter but of course as you say everything must be indefinite until we meet and talk it over. Give my love to dear Dell and tell her I did not tell her in my letter to her for fear it might hurt her, that for the short time I go to town I will stay with Mrs. Mason Smith who has been most kind in urging it. The associations with the house in Legare St. are now so solemn and sacred to me that I do not think I could possibly even put on the outward composure necessary to ordinary life there. Show this to dear Dell and I feel sure she will understand and forgive me. I look forward with great pleasure to seeing the children and came very near making up my mind to take rooms that I saw advertised, without delaying further, but I am very glad I waited for I see my duty quite differently now. Nothing in the world can make me other than miserable this winter and I had better try and be of what use I can without thinking of my likes and dislikes in small matters, and I feel sure that is the only hope for me. Jinty has had the care of two younger children long enough and I want her to have this winter quite free (she w[oul]d be furious if she saw this). Of course dear Mama I will not do anything without your sanction, but I think after talking it over you will let me have my way. I have not spoken of it at all to brother yet. If you still wanted to keep Mary I daresay it would be best, but I think I could take care of the little ones. My health is very good, better than usual for the last two weeks. As for living anywhere just as a guest, that is out of the question. I am naturally morbid, and must feel myself of use or suffer.

I have had two most kind and just letters from Mrs. Pringle and will show them to you with pleasure when you come. Do not get impatient to come down dear Mammy but try and get very strong and well so as to repay us for having been so long without you...

Diary

Chicora Wood Nov. 1st. We have been down here a week today. It is strange to be in this my childhood's home again. I thought I had left the nest forever and lo at the end of a few short years here I am back again, my wings broken and bleeding, thankful to find myself in the old home again, only now it is so full there seems no place for me, tho' everyone is so kind and good to me. I know I will be guided to do what is best for I have no wish in the matter of future home now. I am perfectly willing to go wherever God calls me. It seems to me my duty is to go to Brother but I will not act hastily but go by what Mamma wishes.

The political excitement continues very great. Charley has gone to Georgetown today to hear Gen. Hampton. I trust everything will be quiet. The barbeque on Friday went off very quietly. Mr. Dozier and Col. Richardson spoke very well they say. They spent [Friday] night here. I only saw them in the morning at breakfast, but was not pleased with Mr. Dozier. Tho' evidently a clever man he has not a reliable face. My dear brother Char[ley] looks very badly. I shall be truly thankful when all the election work is over. God in His mercy grant that all may be peaceful.

Lynch came up for a few minutes on Friday and brought my mail. In it came a beautiful book from

Widowhood

Mr. Alston Pringle, scraps of consolation called "Gone Before." Reading it has done me much good. Jinty is not well, sore throat and pains in her bones. I trust it will be nothing more. I am astonishingly well.

Sunday Nov. 5th. A beautiful sunshiny day such as my darling and I would have enjoyed so together, but I feel that he has enjoyments now far beyond my power to understand or imagine. Oh my love, my love, God is very good and leads us with wonderful gentleness. I know that nothing could have detached me from this earth as long as you were here, but now I look with such longing eyes to heaven. Where the treasure is there the heart is and oh what a blessing unspeakable to have one's treasure in Heaven. I only dread that gradually that strong feeling may die out, of nearness to God which my great sorrow has brought.

Nov. 13th Monday. Again comes round the 13th which is the last day which my darling spent with me. Only three months. Oh my beloved how blank life is without you, tho' I try hard to interest myself in things around me, and I think I can say truly that I am cheerful to all outward seeming, within there is such a deadness to everything here. I play with the children and talk with Jane and Charley and all the time it is as tho' my real self were miles away and that was a false self. However God in his mercy has sent me healing and I am much quieter than I was this date a month ago.

I have had two most kind letters from Mrs. Pringle in the [past]. She gives me a warm invitation to spend this summer with her. I wrote her last night. I thought it would be impossible for one year at least. Wrote to Mrs. L[uquer] too to thank her for her kindness about the photograph I received at the White House Friday. I was greatly disappointed in it. They have altered the [nose] entirely but it is a beautiful photograph, clear and distinct.

Charley has been quite ill, a severe cold which fell on his chest. I was much alarmed night before last thinking his lungs were affected. The Doctor has seen him three times and today he is up and out but the Doctor recommends great [sic]. Dear Char[ley] he is very lonely.

Nov. 21st. 3 months today since my own one passed away. Oh my God be merciful to me and keep me in thy love. Let nothing draw my thoughts and hopes from Thee. Let no earthly affection ever more take possession of my heart to make me look on this earth as my home. I try to reconcile myself to having no child by that thought, that if I had one I would not feel detached from earth as I do now. But oh my Father it is very dreary. Sometimes I feel despairing. It is so hard to have faith and believe that Thou will give me strength when thou sendest the burden.

Dear Mamma came home Saturday looking well and strong. July and herself left me together—she weak and suffering, he apparently well.

Chapter Nine:

The Years Beyond

THE DEATH OF JOHN JULIUS PRINGLE, observed Margaretta P. Childs, "was a blow from which Mrs. Pringle never entirely recover 'with broken, trailing wings' she soon returned to Chicora and took up the nearest duties."

Ellen, the wife of Benjamin Allston, had passed away in 1875, and Bessie helped to care for her brother's motherless children until he remarried in 1882. She also helped her mother run Chicora Wood, and when her sister Adele lost her husband in 1881, she assisted in the upbringing of those nieces and nephews, skillfully nursing them and other relations through many illnesses.

In 1879, Bessie received a bequest from a relative which allowed her to purchase White House Plantation. Her brother Charles managed White House for several years, until Bessie took over its management in 1885. After her mother's death in 1896, Chicora Wood had to be sold to pay off debts of the estate. Bessie could not bear to see Chicora Wood go out of the family, so she took out a mortgage on the place and remained there, giving the following details in *Chronicles*:

> None of my family was able to buy it, and a syndicate seemed the only likely purchaser, and they wanted to get it for very little. So I determined the best thing I could do was to buy it myself and devote the rest of my life to keeping it in the family, and perhaps at my death some of the younger generation would be able

to take it. This would condemn me to a very isolated existence, with much hard work and anxiety; but, after all, work is the greatest blessing, as I have found.

For more than a decade following, Bessie planted both plantations with rice and other crops, but she always struggled financially, as rice culture became a doomed enterprise. In 1919, the house at White House Plantation burned, and the following year she sold the property.

In the early twentieth century, she turned to writing as a way of earning more badly needed income. The editor of the *New York Sun* newspaper accepted her proposal to write (under the pen name Patience Pennington) a series of articles recounting her experiences as a widow operating two South Carolina rice plantations, and these were published in that periodical from 1903 to 1912. In 1913, they were transformed into the book *A Woman Rice Planter*. The book did not bring great financial rewards to its author, but it was a critical and popular success, and is considered a classic of its kind. Dr. Anne M. Blythe expounded on the significance of Bessie's work in her introduction to *A Woman Rice Planter:*

> [I]t is the self-portrait of the author which gives the book its greatest distinction and will live the longest in most readers' memories. For it is a full portrait of a woman of integrity and complexity, of great courage and capacity for love, of humor and power and quiet dignity, and of a woman whose religious belief was essential to her whole being and her every act. It is one of the most remarkable of all the surviving pictures we have of the people of her time and place, and it can fairly be said that it shows the culture and society and civilization that produced her at its best.

In 1914 and 1915, she published "Rab and Dab" in three parts in the *Atlantic Monthly* magazine. It was the story of two black orphans who first appeared in *A Woman Rice Planter*. Dr. Anne M. Blythe

The Years Beyond

described this tale of two devilish little boys (whom Bessie tried to help), as a "study in the eternal struggle" between good and evil.[261]

After the publication of *A Woman Rice Planter,* a friend encouraged Bessie to write about her childhood and family, and, making use of diaries and letters, she began to set down her recollections in a book that would become *Chronicles of Chicora Wood,* which was published in 1922 (the year following her death).

As a widow, Bessie had continued to keep a diary, and certain dates would bring bittersweet reflections on her all-too-brief marriage:

> 1879, April 26. The anniversary of my marriage. It is nine years since then and it seems a lifetime. I have done everything as tho' it were a common day with me, but my heart has been heavy. Oh July my darling I miss you so.
>
> 1880, August 21. This day four years ago my darling ceased to breathe. J.P.L. came for me and arrived on the beach about one o'clock and we left at three unconscious that it was already too late, for his noble spirit had passed away before I left the house. Yet I went on feeling sure I would be able to nurse him back to health. God have mercy on me and help me to be good and patient. And God have mercy on him my darling and my love.
>
> 1893, August 21. God help me to live a worthy useful life. That is my prayer now. The seventeen years which are gone since my own passed away seem as nothing as I look back but God has been good to me and helped and guided me. Oh my father lead me on, hold my hand. Sometimes the way seems darker than ever. If only I could keep close to God, but alas, alas for the poor frail human nature.

---

261 Pringle, *Rab and Dab,* xviii.

Bessie in Love and War

> 1912, August 20. Oh my beloved, my beloved, anything that brings you back to me is precious. To think if our child had lived, he would have been forty years old and I might have had grandchildren.[262]

In 1914, Bessie wrote to her friend and fellow author Owen Wister about seeing her husband for the last time in 1876:

> I made the terrible journey to Charleston and stood on tiptoe to look down into the ice-packed coffin where he lay—instead of crying out and fainting as they thought I would, my whole being broke into a smile! Then and there I held communion with the great loving heart of the man I loved, and his spirit calmed and filled mine as it had never succeeded in doing before, his brave and faithful soul permeated mine, his strong courage passed into me, and from that hour my nature was changed—I was not afraid of anything...[263]

Her marriage had been a happy one, and the loss of her husband a devastating blow, but when she looked back across the years, she saw God's hand in her life, and how that blow was used to mold her into a more profitable servant of Christ. In *Chronicles* she reflected:

> Never was a girl more blessed than I in her marriage, too happy to live, I often felt. Alas, my happiness so possessed me that it made me blind to the world outside. What cared I for the world, or outer world, as long as my little paradise was untouched? Alas, it had to go; and so one thing after another had to be taken before this poor piece of humanity was fit for the Master's use, able to yield and to help others to yield. And now I thank the great Father for all that crushing

---

262 Bessie put the following scripture verse (Philippians 1:3) on her husband's gravestone: "I thank my God upon every remembrance of you."

263 Quoted in Anne M. Blythe's introduction to the 1991 edition of *A Woman Rice Planter,* xvii.

THE YEARS BEYOND

and sorrow, as I used as a little child to thank and adore my father for his punishments.

In her widowhood, although her life was not without its pleasures and pursuits of personal interests (including travel and art studies), Bessie lived what Margaretta P. Childs called "a strenuous and sacrificial life." She generously gave of herself to her family, her friends, her community, and her country. Childs wrote of her in this period:

> She was the moving spirit in the extensive repair of old Prince Frederick Church, raising the money and supervising the work. She arranged for the publication of its early register, copying the old manuscript and securing the backing of the State chapter of Colonial Dames. She attended to a voluminous correspondence for the Mt. Vernon Ladies Association which she had wholeheartedly served since 1903 as State Vice-Regent.

The Mount Vernon Ladies' Association, founded in the 1850s by another extraordinary South Carolina woman, Anne Pamela Cunningham, was dedicated to the restoration and preservation of George Washington's estate at Mount Vernon. Bessie was an active, faithful member of the organization up to the time of her death.

In early December 1921, shortly after returning to Chicora Wood from Mount Vernon, Bessie began to suffer serious heart problems. According to one of her obituaries, two days before her death, she sent for her pastor, the Rev. J.E.H. Galbraith, the rector of Prince Frederick's Parish Church, and for William A. Guerry, the bishop of South Carolina, who happened to be in the area. She passed away in the early morning hours of Monday, December 5.[264] Her funeral took place the afternoon of that same day at Prince Frederick's Church,

---

264   Rev. Galbraith wrote this tribute to her: "She never grew old—she loved not in word only, but in deed and truth." Quoted in Anne M. Blythe's introduction to the 1991 edition *A Woman Rice Planter*, xx.

and the next day, her body was taken to Charleston, where she was buried next to her husband at Magnolia Cemetery.[265]

In *A Woman Rice Planter,* Bessie sometimes looked back on her past. Her musings in one particularly poignant passage beautifully sum up her life, and seem a fitting way to close her story here:

> My wedding day thirty-six years ago! It does not seem possible that there can be one atom of the intensely pleasure loving, gay slip of a girl left in the philosopher, who, battered and bruised by life's battle, looks with calm, serene eyes on the stormy path behind her and with absolute faith forward to the sunset hour. It does not seem as though the ego could possibly be the same. Had some magic mirror been possible, in which that girl could have been shown herself, and her solitary life at the end of forty years, she could not have faced life, she would have prayed passionately for death.
>
> Everything she specially cared for and valued has been taken from her, the things she specially disliked and feared have come upon her, and yet all that is great and noble in life, seems nearer to her now. God seems to have turned all the evil into good, all the mud and mire into gold, and there are around her the beautiful mists and clouds of sunset, which is not so far off now. So does the Great Father fuse and mould and change in His mighty workshop. Thank God for His alchemy.

---

[265] According to the interment records of Magnolia Cemetery, her attending physician was Dr. William Minott Gaillard, who listed her cause of death as angina pectoris.

Bibliography

Manuscripts:

Alston-Pringle-Frost Papers (1285.00) South Carolina Historical Society (SCHS)

Allston and Rutledge Families Papers (0487.00) SCHS

Allston Family Papers (1164.00) SCHS

Childs Family Papers (1224.00) SCHS

Elizabeth W. Allston Pringle Family Papers (1003.00) SCHS

Elizabeth Waties Allston Pringle Family Papers (0486.00) SCHS

Elizabeth Waties Allston Pringle Family Papers (0508.00) SCHS

Pringle, Elizabeth W. Allston. "Plantations on the Pee Dee." Vincent P. Lannie Collection, Special Collections, College of Charleston.

Trapier Family Papers, 1861-1910. South Caroliniana Library, University of South Carolina.

Vanderhorst Family Papers. (1169.00) SCHS

Published Primary and Secondary Sources:

Allston, Susan Lowndes. "White House Plantation." *News and Courier,* November 16, 1930.

Blythe, Anne M. *Yours from the Wilderness: Excerpts from the Writings of Elizabeth Allston Pringle*. Columbia, SC: Seajay Press, 1986.

Chambers, Herbert O. *And Were the Glory of Their Times: The Men Who Died for South Carolina in the War for Southern Independence, Cavalry.* Wilmington, NC: Broadfoot Publishing Co., 2015.

Chesnut, Mary Boykin. *A Diary from Dixie.* Cambridge, MA: Harvard University Press, 1980.

Clements, Pamela J. "Great Events have Taken Place": The Civil War Diary of Adele Allston Vanderhorst." *South Carolina Historical Magazine,* 102 (Oct. 2021): 310-334.

Cohen, Henning. *A Barhamville Miscellany.* Columbia: University of South Carolina Press, 1956.

Cote, Richard N. *Mary's World: Love, War, and Family Ties in Nineteenth Century Charleston.* Mount Pleasant, SC: Corinthian Books, 2001.

Darlingtoniana: A History of People, Places and Events in Darlington County, South Carolina. Edited by Eliza Cowan Ervin and Horace Fraser Rudisill. Columbia, SC: The R. L. Bryan Company, 1976.

Davidson, Chalmers Gaston. *The Last Foray: The South Carolina Planters of 1860.* Columbia: University of South Carolina Press, 1971.

Devereux, Anthony Q. *The Life and Times of Robert F.W. Allston.* Georgetown, SC: Waccamaw Press, 1976.

Easterby, J. H., ed. *The South Carolina Rice Plantation as Revealed in the Papers of Robert F. W. Allston.* Columbia: University of South Carolina Press, 2004.

Elmore, Tom. *A Carnival of Destruction: Sherman's Invasion of South Carolina.* Charleston, SC: Joggling Board Press, 2012.

Emerson, W. Eric. *Sons of Privilege: The Charleston Light Dragoons in the Civil War.* Columbia: University of South Carolina Press.

Fenhagen, Mary Pringle. "Descendants of Judge Robert Pringle." *South Carolina Historical Magazine* 62 (Oct. 1961): 221-236.

Kibler, James Everett. *The Classical Origins of Southern Literature, Second Edition.* McClellanville, SC: Abbeville Institute Press, 2023.

Bibliography

Linder, Suzanne Cameron, and Marta Leslie Thacker. *Historical Atlas of the Rice Plantations of Georgetown County and the Santee River*. Columbia: South Carolina Department of Archives and History, 2001.

McGuire, Judith Brockenbrough. *Diary of a Southern Refugee During the War*. Edited by James I. Roberston. Lexington: University Press of Kentucky, 2014.

McInnis, Maurie D., and Angela D. Mack. *In Pursuit of Refinement: Charlestonians Abroad, 1740-1860*. Columbia: University of South Carolina Press, 1999.

Mount Vernon Ladies' Association of the Union. *Annual Report of the Mount Vernon Ladies' Association of the Union, 1921*.

Our Women in the War: The Lives They Lived; The Deaths They Died. Charleston, SC: The News and Courier Book Presses, 1885.

Pease, Jane H., and William H. Pease. *A Family of Women: The Carolina Petigrus in Peace and War*. Chapel Hill: The University of North Carolina Press, 1999.

Powell, William S., ed. *Dictionary of North Carolina Biography*. Chapel Hill: University of North Carolina Press, 1996.

Pringle, Elizabeth Allston. *A Woman Rice Planter*. Columbia, SC: The Seajay Press, 1991.

Pringle, Elizabeth Allston. *Rab and Dab*. Edited by Anne Blythe. Spartanburg, SC: The Reprint Company, 1985.

Pringle, Elizabeth W. Allston. *Chronicles of Chicora Wood*. New York: Charles Scribner's Sons, 1922.

Pringle Elizabeth W. Allston. *A Woman Rice Planter*. Columbia: University of South Carolina Press, 1992.

Scarborough, William K. *The Allstons of Chicora Wood*. Baton Rouge: Louisiana State University Press, 2011.

Shull, Hugh. *A Guide Book of Southern States Currency*. Atlanta, GA: Whitman Publishing, 2007.

Stokes, Karen. *South Carolina Civilians in Sherman's Path: Stories of Courage Amid Civil War Destruction*. Charleston, SC: The History Press, 2012.

Walters, John B. *Merchant of Terror: General Sherman and Total War*. New York: The Bobbs-Merrill Company, 1973.

Wilson, Clyde N. *Carolina Cavalier: The Life and Mind of James Johnston Pettigrew*. Athens: University of Georgia Press, 1990.

ABOUT THE EDITOR

KAREN STOKES, an archivist at the South Carolina Historical Society in Charleston, is the prolific author of over a dozen history books about South Carolina and its people during the War Between the States, all based on primary manuscript sources. These include, among others, *South Carolina Civilians in Sherman's Path, The Immortal 600, A Confederate Englishman, Confederate South Carolina, Days of Destruction, A Legion of Devils: Sherman in South Carolina, Fortunes of War: The Adventures of a German Confederate,* and *A Confederate in Paris: Letters of A. Dudley Mann 1867-1879.* She has also written works of historical fiction published by Green Altar (an imprint of Shotwell Publishing) including *Belles, Carolina Love Letters, The Immortals,* and *Honor in the Dust.*

Best Sellers and New Releases

Over 90 Titles For You To Enjoy

THE SOUTH'S FINEST CONTEMPORARY AUTHORS.

Shotwell Publishing is proud to be called home by many of today's most respected Southern scholars and literary greats.

JEFFERY ADDICOTT
Union Terror: Debunking the False Justifications for Union Terror

Trampling Union Terror: Riders of the Second Alabama Cavalry

MARK ATKINS
Women in Combat: Feminism Goes to War

JOYCE BENNETT
Maryland, My Maryland: The Cultural Cleansing of a Small Southern State

GARRY BOWERS
Slavery and The Civil War: What Your History Teacher Didn't Tell You

Dixie Days: Reminiscences Of a Southern Boyhood

JERRY BREWER
Dismantling the Republic

ANDREW P. CALHOUN
My Own Darling Wife: Letters From A Confederate Volunteer

JOHN CHODES
Segregation: Federal Policy or Racism?

Washington's KKK: The Union League During Southern Reconstruction

WALTER BRIAN CISCO
War Crimes Against Southern Civilians

DAVID T. CRUM
Stonewall Jackson: Saved by Providence

STEPHEN DAVIS
Confederate Triumph: How the South Won Its War for Independence 1861-1863 Volume One:1861

JOHN DEVANNY
Continuities: The South in a Time of Revolution

Lincoln's Continuing Revolution: Essays of M.E. Bradford and Thomas H. Landess

JOSHUA DOGGRELL
Doxed: The Political Lynching of a Southern Cop

JAMES C. EDWARDS
What Really Happened?: Quantrill's Raid On Lawrence, Kansas

TED EHMANN
Boom & Bust In Bone Valley: Florida's Phosphate Mining History 1886-2021

JOHN AVERY EMISON
The Deep State Assassination of Martin Luther King Jr.

DON GORDON
Snowball's Chance: My Kidneys Failed, My Wife Left Me & My Dog Died...

JOHN R. GRAHAM
Constitutional History of Secession

PAUL C. GRAHAM
Confederaphobia

When The Yankees Come: Former Carolina Slaves Remember

JOE D. HAINES
The Diary of Col. John Henry Stover Funk of the Stonewall Brigade, 1861-1862

CHARLES HAYES
The REAL First Thanksgiving

V.P. HUGHES
Col. John Singleton Mosby: In the News 1862-1916

TERRY HULSEY
25 Texas Heroes

The Constitution of Non-State Government: Field Guide to Texas Secession

JOSEPH JAY
Sacred Conviction: The South's Stand for Biblical Authority

JAMES R. KENNEDY
Dixie Rising: Rules For Rebels

Nullifying Federal and State Gun Control: A How-To Guide For Gun Owners

When Rebel Was Cool: Growing Up In Dixie, 1950-1965

Reconstruction: Destroying the Republic and Creating an Empire

WALTER D. KENNEDY
The South's Struggle: America's Hope

Lincoln, The Non-Christian President: Exposing The Myth

Lincoln, Marx, and the GOP

J.R. & W.D. KENNEDY
Jefferson Davis: High Road to Emancipation and Constitutional Government

Yankee Empire: Aggressive Abroad and Despotic at Home

Punished With Poverty: The Suffering South

The South Was Right! 3rd Edition

LEWIS LIBERMAN
Snowflake Buddies; ABC Leftism For Kids!

PHILIP LEIGH
The Devil's Town: Hot Springs During The Gangster Era

U.S. Grant's Failed Presidency

The Causes of the Civil War

The Dreadful Frauds: Critical Race Theory And Identity Politics

JACK MARQUARDT
Around The World In 80 Years: Confessions of a Connecticut Confederate

MICHAEL MARTIN
Southern Grit: Sensing The Siege at Petersburg

SAMUEL MITCHAM
The Greatest Lynching In American History: New York, 1863

Confederate Patton: Richard Taylor and The Red River Campaign

CHARLES T. PACE
Lincoln As He Really Was

Southern Independence. Why War? The War To Prevent Southern Independence

JAMES R. ROESCH
From Founding Fathers To Fire Eaters

KIRKPATRICK SALE
Emancipation Hell: The Tragedy Wrought By Lincoln's Emancipation Proclamation

JOSEPH SCOTCHIE
The Asheville Connection: The Making of a Conservative

Samuel T. Francis and Revolution from the Middle

ANNE W. SMITH
Charlottesville Untold: Inside Unite The Right

Robert E. Lee: A History for Kids

KAREN STOKES
A Legion Of Devils: Sherman In South Carolina

The Burning of Columbia, S.C.: A Review of Northern Assertions and Southern Facts

Carolina Love Letters

Fortunes of War: The Adventures of a German Confederate

A Confederate in Paris: Letters of A. Dudley Mann 1867-1879

JOSEPH R. STROMBERG
Southern Story and Song: Country Music in the 20th Century

JACK TROTTER
Last Train to Dixie

JOHN THEURSAM
Key West's Civil War

H.V. TRAYWICK, JR.
Along The Shadow Line: A Road Trip through History and Memory on the Old Confederate Border

LESLIE TUCKER
Old Times There Should Not Be Forgotten: Cultural Genocide In Dixie

JOHN VINSON
Southerner Take Your Stand!

MARK R. WINCHELL
Confessions of a Copperhead: Culture and Politics in the Modern South

CLYDE N. WILSON
Calhoun: A Statesman for the 21st Century

Lies My Teacher Told Me: The True History of the War For Southern Independence

The Yankee Problem: An American Dilemma

Annals Of The Stupid Party: Republicans Before Trump

Nullification: Reclaiming The Consent of the Governed

The Old South: 50 Essential Books

The War Between The States: 60 Essential Books

Reconstruction and the New South, 1865-1913: 50 Essential Books

The South 20th Century And Beyond: 50 Essential Books

Southern Poets and Poems, 1606-1860: The Land They Loved, Volume 1

Confederate Poets and Poems, Vol1 The Land They Loved, Volume II

Looking For Mr. Jefferson

African American Slavery in Historical Perspective

JOE WOLVERTON
What Degree Of Madness?: Madison's Method To Make American States Again

WALTER KIRK WOOD
Beyond Slavery: The Northern Romantic Nationalist Origins of America's Civil War

SHOTWELLPUBLISHING.COM

Green Altar (Literary Imprint)

CATHARINE SAVAGE BROSMAN
*An Aesthetic Education
and Other Stories (2nd Ed)*

Chained Tree, Chained Owls: Poems

Aerosols and Other Poems

Partial Memoirs

RANDALL IVEY
*A New England Romance:
And Other Southern Stories*

The Gift of Gab

SUZANNE JOHNSON
Maxcy Gregg's Sporting Journals 1842-1858

JAMES E. KIBLER, JR.
Tiller : Claybank County Series, Vol. 4

The Gentler Gamester

*Beyond The Stone: Poems of Tribute
& Remembrance*

THOMAS MOORE
*A Fatal Mercy:
The Man Who Lost The Civil War*

PERRIN LOVETT
The Substitute, Tom Ironsides 1

KAREN STOKES
Belles

Carolina Twilight

Honor in the Dust

The Immortals

The Soldier's Ghost: A Tale of Charleston

WILLIAM THOMAS
*Runaway Haley:
An Imagined Family Saga*

*The Field of Justice: Moonshine
and Murder in North Georgia*

CLYDE N. WILSON
*Southern Poets and Poems, 1606-1860:
The Land They Loved, Volume 1*

*Confederate Poets and Poems, Vol 1
The Land They Loved, Volume II*

Gold-Bug
(Mystery & Suspense Imprint)

BRANDI PERRY
Splintered: A New Orleans Tale

MARTIN WILSON

Free Book Offer

Don't get left out, y'all.
Sign-up and be the first to know about new releases, sales, and other goodies
—plus we'll send you TWO FREE EBOOKS!

Lies My Teacher Told Me:
The True History of the War for Southern Independence
by Dr. Clyde N. Wilson

When The Yankees Come
Former Carolina Slaves Remember Sherman's March From the Sea
by Paul C. Graham

FreeLiesBook.com

Southern Books. No Apologies.
We love the South — its history, traditions, and culture — and are proud of our inheritance as Southerners. Our books are a reflection of this love.

www.ingramcontent.com/pod-product-compliance
Lightning Source LLC
Chambersburg PA